THE GAMES OF MAYA

Delia Steinberg Guzmán

First published in Spanish under the title *Los Juegos de Maya* (Editorial NA. Madrid, 2001. 1st Ed. 1980).

Translated from Spanish by Julian Scott.

Published in 2025 by

NEW ACROPOLIS

New Acropolis Cultural Organization

Mumbai, India.
www.acropolis.org.in
mumbai@acropolis.org.in

ISBN: 978-81-964729-3-1

Printed in India.

THE GAMES OF MAYA

Delia Steinberg Guzmán

CONTENTS

PROLOGUE

However deeply we dive into the knowledge of the human past, we will always find the human being with his natural philosophical wonder at the nature of the world around him and his own nature. His questions rise up to the sky like the smoke of incense burners; born from a burning fire and pulled upwards by an attraction away from the earth, which is proper to the non-material nature of his ancestral being.

The detailed observation of his environment reveals the fleeting nature of things. And even though his questions fade into mystery without obtaining any concrete answers, somehow he knows that he remains and will always remain beyond the kaleidoscopic glass bead game of the objects he perceives.

From this arises the view of life as a game in which everything is important and, at the same time, is not. The perception of this lack of metaphysical importance has inspired a book written with poetry and simplicity – "The Games of Maya" – for which I am writing this prologue.

As its author is my disciple on the paths of philosophy, it is not for me to issue a stream of praise which arises sincerely from the depths of my soul, but I can state that it is very difficult to say such profound things as Delia S. Guzmán has said in such clear and accessible words. More than words, she has written steps, which the reader will find easy to follow and will lead him or her, as in a children's dance, to the joy of not experiencing life or nature as enemies, but as allies that God has placed on our path to awaken our consciousness.

The many themes that are touched upon are joined by a single thread that points towards unity, infusing every chapter with vitality. But the optimistic tone is never lost and, on the great chess board of reality, the moving pieces slide, now here, now there, in the great game of Maya, where the important thing is not who wins, but to play. Because this is what enables us to feel alive and gather experience.

"The Games of Maya" is, in brief, a short, concise book in the core of its philosophical content, but extremely light and easy to assimilate.

With its help, readers will learn to "play at life" without painful effort, and to ask themselves the most fundamental questions in a natural way; questions which, as we mentioned earlier, rise up to the sky like smoke from the incense burners of old, like an age-old prayer repeated by new lips, just when the world most needs space, simplicity and a healthy enjoyment of life.

Jorge A. Livraga Rizzi
Founder of New Acropolis International

INTRODUCTION

Maya is an ancient oriental deity whose name means illusion. She is the veil with which Nature covers all things so that we humans cannot easily discover her hidden laws. In this way, the beauty of Maya and her manifold games beguile us, seduce us and help us to pass the years of life which are allotted to us on this Earth.

Illusion plays with our senses and, more or less consciously, we join in the game. Illusion is not exactly something that does not exist, because we can perceive it. The games of illusion are based on real, but not permanent things; they are truths that live for as long as a bubble – or an illusion – lives. But we, in our ignorance, assume that those momentary truths are everything.

It is by focusing our efforts and our highest hopes on the games of Maya that we come to know pain. Everything we want slips through our fingers, and we become blind to the possibility of seeing other things that are more lasting, less fallible, closer to immortality.

Why do we play? Why do we accept the illusion of Maya without realizing it? To answer this question would be equivalent to knowing precisely why children play. They play, even though they know that the games they are playing are not real; but they need to practise, to test their abilities and prepare themselves for the greater game, which is life itself.

We humans are always a little like children. Uncertain of the final destiny that awaits us, we play in life, trying to prove to ourselves that we are capable of achieving things. All of us are taking part in the "Games of Maya".

THE GAME

Once upon a time there was a very serious child, so serious that he felt deeply sorry for the other children who spent their days playing. This child had noticed that the dolls, the toy cars, the masks and all the other toys, were treated by the grown-ups as worthless and unreal. And so, not wanting to be less than them, he decided to do without these illusions as well.

While all the children played, the child of our story remained solitary and aloof, suffering as he watched his poor companions enjoying their games and imaginary adventures. The solitary child tried to find consolation in reading, but he soon saw that books too were filled with fantasies and stories that were not always true. The child then turned to the contemplation of nature, and discovered to his horror that nature too was playing... beguiling and deceiving with lights and colours, shapes and perfumes.

The child needed an explanation, so he went back to his former playmates, and asked them:

'Why are you playing? Can't you see that all your toys are not real, that they are of no use to you in real life?'

'We are playing at being grown-ups.'

'But your cars are not like grown-ups' cars... you can't drive them in the streets... And your dolls are not like real children.'

'We know that. But while we are using these little cars and these little dolls, we are practising what we will do when we will be grown-up men and women. Then we won't be afraid of having children or driving cars if we need to.'

'So you know you are playing with illusions?'

'Of course we know, but we don't think about it. If we were to be constantly reminding ourselves that our toys are imitations, we wouldn't be able to play. And we need to play, we need to rehearse what we will be doing tomorrow in reality. That's why we throw ourselves into our games and enjoy them as if they were real.'

The solitary child retraced his steps and understood the reason for his eternal sadness. It doesn't always bring happiness to know the truth about everything or to be continually aware of the truths of life.

***

Once upon a time there was a man whom everyone called a "philosopher". He was different from others and was not interested in the same things; in fact, he felt a great contempt for the day-to-day concerns of "normal" human beings. The philosopher knew things about life and death, about good and evil, about destiny and its laws, and wanted nothing to do with the vanities of the world.

While all the other humans rushed about like industrious

little ants, our philosopher remained aloof, thoughtful and solitary, suspicious of the feelings, thoughts and intentions of everyone else.

He watched others with an ironic smile. How could they fail to realize that they were taking part in the great game of life? Couldn't they see that all their efforts were in vain, as the destiny of humanity was already traced in the stars. How could they suffer and laugh, worry and desire, without understanding that nothing was worth laughter or tears, desire or longing?

For the "philosopher", to eat was a torture; to sleep, a necessity of the body; to love, little more than a lack of maturity and self-sufficiency. To read, futile; to act, unnecessary. To suffer... something which not even he could avoid with all his philosophy. And that made him terribly similar to the rest...

***

For Maya and her games are also one of the laws of life. One thing is to know her traps, but it is a very different matter to want to escape from them. To become aware of the game of Maya is to acquire human consciousness. To escape from the games of Maya is equivalent to being much more than a simple philosopher: it is to have reached God, it is to have taken a leap beyond the human level and its needs.

As long as we exist at this stage of evolution, Maya will be our inseparable companion. She not only tries to deceive us, but also to lend beauty, with her veils and smiles, to the harsh experiences through which we all have to pass if we really want to overcome ourselves. There is more kindness than malice in Maya, more desire to help than to harm. And it is also up to human beings to notice and be grateful for this effort of Nature to make our life on Earth more pleasant to bear.

To play, without forgetting what we are doing: that is the secret; to prepare ourselves for "when we are grown-up", for when we will no longer need toys or props to unfold our potential; but in the meantime, to accept our condition as children, and try to grow; with Maya at our side, with her games and ambushes, her enchantments and her traps, with the flavours that make life pass quickly and add new and important experiences to our knowledge. For knowledge allows us to see things free from evil and ugliness. With knowledge, the games of Maya are the spice of life.

***

As I write this, I remember that when I was little and weary of the demands of social convention, I often used to imagine that life was a great game, a great drama on the stage of existence. Then, I took delight in each of my actions, imagining that I was an actress and that I had to play my part in the best possible way, as thousands of eyes were watching me. And I played at acting, paying attention to my clothes and my gestures, my glances and my movements.

In adolescence, I threw aside the illusion of the theatre and its stage... Life was something too serious and important to be playing at it.

And now, I have returned to the principles which inspired me in my childhood. All this is a great game. Maya, her toys, all human beings and I myself, are the actors. Life is the stage. When the curtain falls and the lights go out, the performance will end, and the doors of a new mystery will open. And I am not sure that Maya will not be there as well, in the shadows of the curtains, awaiting us with new toys to help us live in that other new world.

SOLITUDE

If we imagine existence as a sine wave, there will be moments that can be seen above the midline, which we call moments of life; and there will be others that lie below the horizon: these we call death. In reality, everything is existence, whether on one side or the other of the dividing line. The crucial moment is when we cross this line, whether at the moment of birth or at the moment of death.

Both when we are born and when we die, we are alone. It doesn't matter how many people are around us at those times: ultimately, we are alone. And most probably we are alone throughout the whole of our life. Not because we can't share our time with others, but because, deep down, nobody can enter into our soul, which is also solitary by nature.

It is difficult to unveil the mystery of life and death. If death, because of our ignorance, is something that frightens us, life and the reason we came into this life will continue to be nearly insoluble questions for the human mind.

It is likely that, at a certain moment, our soul detached itself from something much greater which contained it. It detached itself in search of new experiences, guided by the innocent lack of knowledge that characterizes young souls. In this way, it came to earth alone, terribly alone, torn from its celestial womb. Since then, it has been roaming the earth, sometimes with a covering of matter, at other times without, in search of the key that will enable it to return to its primal origin, where it was not alone, because it was not separated. That key is knowledge. To know is to be able to act. Someday, just as we left, we will be able to return.

***

Solitude is one of Maya's great allies. The more alone we feel, the more we take refuge in the games of illusion, in an attempt to remove this sensation of inner anguish.

Thus, a new drama begins: the drama of living together. Solitary souls who want to live together with other solitary souls, even if they never manage to understand each other completely, since we all bear the mark of solitude.

Living together with others creates a variety of forms, from the simple love that unites two beings to the more complex feelings that characterize society and even humanity. Families, groups, cities, businesses, churches and political parties appear. All these are webs of Maya into which human beings fall and get trapped, believing that, at last, they have overcome their loneliness. But the further they fall, the more lonely they become.

***

The wise Plato said that the human being is made of "the one and the other". Nothing could be more true. The one is the indivisible that lies hidden within, the solitary soul; the other is the mask that goes out into the world and connects with others in multiple ways in order to escape solitude.

When we are wearing our masks, we can play at many forms of companionship. This is the origin of friendship, love, filial and parental sentiments, affection for all human beings, as well as animals and plants. On more subtle levels, love turns towards the infinity of the stars, and human beings even become capable of perceiving God and loving Him because of the perfection they can see in His world.

But how many disappointments we suffer! Friendships that fail, loves that die with time, children who betray their parents, parents who abandon their children, people who care nothing for others... There is a science that makes the romantic brightness of the stars seem cold and there are many religions that fight one another in the name of the same God. What can we do?

That is when people throw away their external masks in disgust and, in desperation, turn inwards, thinking that they will never be able to escape from solitude. And it is here that the great surprise arises.

It is in the human being's own self, in our inner being, that we find a true friend, one that always accompanies us, that is always present and unchanging, in suffering and in joy, that observes our lives without judging us, pulling us upward, always upward, without asking for anything in return.

The miracle continues. When we discover this true friend, parent and brother or sister, everything becomes meaningful again. Reading, listening to music and enjoying the song of Nature are no longer actions of absorbed solitude, but of a person accompanied by their true self.

Now it is possible to make contact with other human beings, since in every one of them, there is another accompanying self with similar interests to those of the friend we have just discovered. Now, understanding and fellow feeling are possible. Someone who has not begun to search within will find it hard to gain even the slightest knowledge of what is outside himself. First, we must go within, then we can go outside.

It is not that solitude will disappear, it is a state proper to the soul. But it will be possible to join solitudes and play with the veils of Maya as long as life continues. Sharing a misfortune is a form of union. And it is even likely that souls will want to come together in the face of the shared misfortune of having lost their primal origin, in their ardent desire to return to that point where there is no longer any division.

***

Solitude is a product of division. When everything is one, what room is there for solitude? Solitude, then, is separation, disunity, division.

The more we divide, the more solitude there is, because we have created new particles that are, in their turn, solitary and separated from the rest.

This is one of the games of Maya: infinitely dividing, multiplying forms and encouraging us to do the same, making us believe that we will find the remedy for solitude in quantity.
But quantity will not bring solitude to an end: when there are

many things, they turn into a heap and there is a loss of quality, because from a single essence come many presences. It is better to look for less quantity and more quality, something that has both depth and height.

It is possible that in this way, by knowing the game of Maya, we may be able to go beyond the illusion and recognize the missing pieces of our soul, those which it lost in its descent to earth and those which it needs to recover in order to re-become one and never feel alone again.

'Are you alone?'

'Yes...'

'Would you like to be with me?'

'Okay...'

And now there are two, walking hand in hand, their masks of flesh united, while their souls peer out curiously into each other's eyes to see if in that being is their twin self, which they lost in that first division.

LIFE AND DEATH

“Oh joy! What happiness! A child has been born! Our child has come into the world!”

This is how people celebrate the appearance of a new human being on earth. Nothing seems too much for this small body that needs the most absolute protection and the most affectionate care. Kisses, gifts and tears of joy and emotion mark this life event.

***

“What terrible pain! How much sorrow I feel in my soul! I have just lost a loved one!”

That is how we human beings mourn the disappearance of those who have accompanied us, as they plunge into that dark mystery of death. Tears of sadness, grief and desolation mark the passing of a soul from one world to the other.

Rarely do we stop to think about where we have come from when we are born. I am not talking about the religious or philosophical question of the origin of souls. It is something simpler: if we come into this life, we have arrived from somewhere else, wherever that may be. Is it not possible that we have left sad and mournful beings in that other place, when we left it to go to the land of the living? What our parents celebrate with joy – will that not then be suffering for those other immaterial parents who are separated from a soul that had accompanied them up to that moment?

And when we die, leaving the earth, where are we going? If we come from somewhere else, we must also be going somewhere else. There can be no defined limits in infinity. And in that place where we are going, won't they welcome us there with the smiles and joy of a reunion, at the same time as our relatives are weeping for us on earth?

***

Life and death are two sides of the same coin: LIFE. Those who are here came from somewhere else, and we are going towards somewhere else, but we will never cease to be.

What human beings call life is the manifested appearance in matter of a soul on this earth. What human beings call death is that same soul which, divested of its matter, cannot survive in this world and sets out for another.

Earthly life is the realm of form. And it is here that Maya becomes strong and confident. She plays with life, she plays with forms, changing and adapting them in order to achieve her goal: more material life, more forms, more multiplication.

When forms first appear in the world of Maya, they are small in size. It is how illusion protects young bodies. No one can fail to feel compassion and tenderness for a small living being. A baby, a small animal, a flower just beginning to open... all elicit care and affection. People not only feel love for their own little children, but also for small animals, however dangerous they may become later. A large tiger is not the same as a little tiger cub; one is wild and terrifying; the other is tender and soft. Even animals are moved by small children, and the same wild beast that will attack an adult human will protect that person's babies, because Maya covers the raging eyes with the blindfold of compassion: life must be saved at any cost; those forms required too much effort and patience for them to be destroyed by a single swipe of a claw.

When forms reach their maturity in the world of Maya, they can already look after themselves and then they no longer arouse feelings of tenderness, but of competition. It is the struggle for survival, where the strong overcome the weak. Love may soften this struggle, but in truth, everything is a question of strength, whether physical, psychological, mental or spiritual. And the strongest always wins, in whatever field it may be. The sporting competitions that people find so entertaining are a replication of that other game of Maya, which is expressed in the competition of everyday life.

Before the forms begin to decline and get worn out, they must fulfil the fundamental duty that Maya imposes on them: to continue producing forms. Using a thousand veils and tricks, Maya will ensure that new bodies come into material life, and for this she needs to make use of those that already exist. The natural egoism of the living would have prevented them from ever reproducing, if it were not for the game of Maya, the deception of pleasure, the illusion that it is oneself who has taken the decision to procreate.
Then comes the decay of forms. This is the final stage; the one which people call old age. Old things no longer inspire

tenderness, nor do they call for competition. They are dry and worn-out things that need replacement. It is a good farewell to life, so that we don't fall in love too much with the brilliance of forms. The soul itself asks to throw off the worn-out shell, in order to recover in another ideal place, the lightness and charm that a heavy body can no longer radiate. Maya herself accelerates the process with a kind of apathy and endless daydreaming, but she never wastes energies, because old forms will be renewed in the depths of the earth or the fragility of ashes. Nothing is lost: everything is transformed.

Life and death are two sides of the same coin, two moments in a perpetual game that repeats itself, producing what human beings call cycles.

Everything in Nature plays in circles: day and night, sun and moon, summer and winter, sleep and wakefulness, childhood and old age. If everything revolves, if everything returns, if the same trees that were once dry are now clothed in green, and the same sea that was once calm now swells with powerful currents, why should we human beings escape from this game?

There is no such thing as chance. There is a perpetual game of Maya, operating under the law of cause and effect, which attracts us and obliges us to undergo our own experience. To live and die blindly, while playing with Maya... or to live and die knowing the rules of the game... That is a question of evolution.

STONES

Maya places so many little toys at our disposal that we tend to forget the deeper meaning of life and judge the value of things by their forms.

Our attitude to stones is an example of this. Until recently they were regarded – and still are, by many – as inanimate objects. People just think of them as things to be used for multiple purposes.

From the stones used to build houses and temples to those used to make roads, from the stones that are transformed into practical tools to those that, when well-carved, are turned into beautiful and useful ornaments for the body – all of them are currently seen as cold and dead, and we use them as if life owes them to us in recognition of all the work we do.

Nevertheless, stones are alive. If we were aware of this, perhaps we would never use them. That is why Maya has given stones the appearance of being inert, thus concealing the wonderful law of resistance that characterizes them.

There are bodies that express themselves through growth and expansion; others do so through resistance. In reality, these two laws are present in all bodies, but combined in different proportions: when the law of growth prevails, we see movement; when what we perceive is non-movement, it is the law of resistance that prevails.

The will of the stone consists in resisting. It keeps its molecules tightly bound together, preventing them from breaking apart and dispersing. It is then that we speak of "hard stones". The greater the resistance, the harder the stone. The harder the stone, the greater the will. The greater the will, the more life there is inside.

***

Despite the game of Maya and the veil she uses to make stones look dead, it is easy to glimpse the truth of the matter.

We can see that the stones around us are not all the same or of the same nature.

There are some – as we were saying – that are softer, and others that are harder, some have more will to resist, while others have less. There are some that are duller and others that are brighter, due to their varying capacities for allowing light to pass through them. There are some that are more highly organized internally and others that are less so, and we can see that the atoms of the former are arranged in such a mathematical way that their geometry amazes us; in such cases we refer to them as "precious stones". There are some that are found in one part of the Earth, while others appear somewhere else; some are formed in "fertile" areas of the Earth, where the energy is stronger and more accessible; others are formed anywhere and anyhow; there are 'bastard' stones as well.

There are stones whose destiny is simply to follow the law of cycles and let the wind erode them until they turn into sand. There are others whose destiny is to yield meekly in human hands and become immortalized in masterpieces. But whether we are talking about a huge stone block in a pyramid or the finest desert sand, all share the same nature of passive but strong resistance.

Stones form part of the game of Maya, as they have a body – and no more than a body. A body like yours and mine, though configured in a different way. Much of our body is made of the same substance as the rock on which we stand. But whereas in us other principles have awakened – psyche, mind, some spirit – in the stone only the body is manifested; the other principles remain dormant. They are awaiting new and distant times when inertia will gradually give way to movement. Then the stone will grow and expand, and a new dimension will begin for it in the eternal illusion of life.

***

When you hear people saying that the sun heats stones and causes them to expand, just pause for a moment. Observe them: they are alive. The same sun that nourishes us also causes changes in the stones.

When you hear people saying that the cold of the night causes stones to contract, don't just carry on as usual, but think: they are alive; they shrink their bodies to withstand the low temperatures. Expansion and contraction are signs of what will later become the movements of the heart.

Stones have a heart too. When you walk on them, or when you caress them gently with your hand, remember that you are in the presence of a living being, which possesses the infinite patience of resistance and waiting.

Remember the ancient sages who, with their great knowledge of the inner life of stones and metals, chose the most suitable ones to create their amulets and talismans. Recall the kings and priests of old, adorned with jewels, which were not worn for the hollow purpose of adornment, but for the deeper reason of capturing and emitting energies.

The fact that stones resist means that they have the ability to retain for many thousands of years the internal strength given to them by their mother, the Earth, and their father, the heavenly bodies.

Talk to the stones and play with them. They will give you an ancient lesson in steadfastness and strength. They will speak to you of other times and other worlds. They will speak to you in vibrant words that will filter through their cracks. With your stone fingers, those fingers of your body which is also matter, speak to the stones.

PLANTS

In plants too there is life and a marvellous principle of intelligence. And Maya plays with them as well, since she needs to perpetuate and multiply the forms of this kingdom of green.

Like stones, plants are children of earth and sky; searching for the mystery of the earth, the roots plunge deep into the soil and, as they drink in the influences of the stars, branches, flowers and fruits emerge.

In plants, the two forces – the force of resistance and the force of expansive growth – begin to become balanced. They grow and open up to the sun, but their roots remain attached to Mother Earth, in an act of pure resistance. By putting down their roots, they are able to withstand winds and storms; divested of leaves, they sleep in winter, and covered in foliage, they defend themselves from the scorching rays of the summer sun. But they live, reveal themselves, move and enjoy their own existence, in an anticipation of what humans do in their own particular way.

Plants are not all the same; even in this world, the differences in degree imposed by evolution are evident. There are very simple plants, small and with minimal expressions, and there are large and robust ones, like trees, that strive to resemble human beings.

Have you ever observed a tree closely? Its trunk is like our body. From this trunk emerge simple feet that sink into the earth and simple arms that rise up towards the sky. The feet are the roots; they are feet that do not walk, but instead seek to attach themselves firmly to their world with the greatest intelligence; today I saw a tree growing among rocks, its roots skilfully making their way through the cracks so as to avoid encountering the hardness of the stone. These root-feet also make a way for themselves, like ours do; but it is a path of stability; food depends on stability and life itself depends on food.

The branches are the arms, full of green fingers. Trees – the most evolved of plants – are always at prayer. They worship the sky and the stars, bless the wind that caresses them and talk to the birds and insects that visit them.

Trees don't have heads... They haven't yet developed the capacity for thought, but they do feel. Despite the deceptions of Maya, there are more and more people who know that plants vibrate and understand the emotions we emit. The beauty of a houseplant largely depends on our skill and affection in caring for it.

Plants do not have heads, but they have obediently received the intelligence that God has placed in them. The flower dresses itself in a variety of colours because it has listened to the voices of Maya, knowing that without this allure, there would be no new flowers. The flower softens the hearts of the wind and the birds, and both wind and birds cooperate in the game of love between the flowers. Pollen travels from one place to another; seeds come and go, and the eternal game of life repeats itself so that the green forms of plant life are never absent from the Earth.

Leaves live from the sun; they point their faces towards the solar king and keep their lungs facing downwards, protecting themselves as they breathe from the dust raised by the wind. Leaves know how to live and how to die; they fall to the ground when golden, creating a harmonious dance as they fall and following the wise selection that first lets go of the older and lower branches, so that the younger and higher ones may endure and stay alive.

The flower also lives from the sun and moves its petals continuously so that it can enrich itself with that gold from the sky. And then, when it has completed its cycle of colour, when everything in it appears to die, it will give rise to the fruit that will have been born from the sacrifice of the flower. And when the fruit withers and destruction takes hold of it, this new sacrifice will give rise to the cyclical seed which, as it falls to the ground, will produce new roots, new trunks, new arms uplifted in prayer and new prayers that are heard, which will be flowers and fruits.

***

Hidden within plants are immeasurable secrets. They possess fantastic virtues which we humans, blinded by the game of Maya, have forgotten how to appreciate. We often eat plants, yet we know very little about the characteristics of what we have just eaten. Some are healing, others are poisonous; they are neither good nor bad, they simply have those properties. Some facilitate dreams and others cause nightmares; some fruits are sweet and pleasant, while others are sour and disgusting. But every plant has a purpose, each has a function and fulfils it conscientiously, whether or not we are aware of these functions.

The sages of antiquity learned how to talk to plants and knew about their many virtues and wondrous properties. In this way, they were wise, while we, on the other hand, are victims of the games of Maya. They crafted strange potions, and we only know of the futile sacrifice of a flower in a vase.

Plants are not solitary beings. On the contrary, many creatures live in them and through them! A careful inspection will reveal hundreds of insects walking among their branches or visiting their roots and, of course, creeping among the colourful flowers and fruits. An attentive ear will discover the songs of birds which make themselves invisible in their foliage; and how can one imagine a tree without a nest? Trees are the homes of birds and, as the sun begins to set, the endless spectacle of birds swiftly seeking shelter in the branches begins.

We human beings – when the game of Maya allows us – are also friends of plants. We coexist with them; we are nourished by them; we use them for decoration and to perfume our homes. We walk among them and are grateful for their benevolent shade in summer, as well as their momentary protection in winter rains.

And there are even beings invisible to our eyes that dwell in the plants, little immaterial gnomes that seek refuge among the branches and worship with true gratitude the being of the tree that gives them shelter.

***

Have you ever noticed how warm wood is? Cradles are made of wood, and so are coffins. There is in wood something of life and something of death, something of movement and something of rest: they are reflections of the resistance and expansion of plants.

When you can stop for a moment and run your hands over your chair or your desk, feeling the warmth of the wood under your fingers, remember that it was once a living being that offered its strength and resistance to continue to be useful, beyond the games of Maya, in the games and works of human beings.

ANIMALS

Because of the pre-eminence of feelings in this realm of Nature, human beings have the most varied emotions about animals. They are feared, loved or regarded with indifference, but they are seldom admired, which is strange, because we only need to observe the display that Maya has made available to this special form of life to be struck with wonder.

When we judge animals, we tend to look at them from two extreme points of view: either they are dangerous wild beasts which we must either escape from or try to kill, or they are inferior beings (to human beings, of course), which we can dominate and exploit. In between, all shades of opinion are possible: apart from those who hunt to eat, there are others who enjoy practising their aim on a living body; there are even those who torture animals because their particular form of cowardice prevents them from confronting other humans who are stronger than themselves.

But did Nature place animals in the world just to frighten or serve human beings? And does Maya deploy her inventiveness just to give an economic incentive to human beings?

Let us see whether there is something more behind the veils of illusion.

***

People say that animals don't have a mind, that they can't reason. In principle, this is true, but maybe it is for the better. Because animals get more benefit than harm from their lack of reasoning.

Without the mind, instincts and feelings arise in animals in a simple and natural way.

On the instinctive level, animals have to eat, stay alive, reproduce, care for their offspring for a time and know how to die with dignity when the time comes.

There are animals that eat until they are more than full; but it is not exactly a vice that makes them behave like that, but rather a kind of economical instinct that obliges them to store up food for "when there is nothing". Some store food in caves and crevices; others do so in their own stomachs, or in special pouches that Maya has made on the sides of their mouths. The gluttony of humans is unknown to animals; there is the instinct to eat, but not vice. If animals kill to eat, at least they don't do it for pleasure; it is necessity that drives them.

Animals attack to defend themselves, not to challenge others. They defend themselves or their offspring, but if they see no danger in humans, it is rare for them to harm or kill. There is an instinct to defend themselves, but not the sport of killing.

To preserve their lives, Maya has provided animals with a thousand and one disguises that allow them to blend in with the colours of Nature, enabling them to survive in the midst of their natural animal enemies and human foes. Have you never seen insects whose colours merge with the surrounding foliage? Or the eyes of owls at night, which blend in with the fireflies? Have you not noticed the striped skins of tigers and cats, which pass unnoticed among the branches of trees?

Maya helps them all... and yet, the big fish eat the small ones. In the whole of Nature, there is an apparent cruelty, which is only another of the illusory games of survival. Strength wins. But each animal has a characteristic that allows it to defend itself from the stronger ones; none of them are helpless or devoid of protection. It is all a question of making use of the skills they have.

All animals have the fundamental instinct to reproduce, from the smallest insects to the most evolved mammals. However, if we look at those mammals in the light of their greater similarity to human nature, we will see that, once again, there is instinct but no vice or passion. Animals mate and reproduce during the time of year that is most appropriate for the development of their offspring. At these times, they seek their mates and no force can deter them from this purpose. However, once the season is over, the animal returns to its peaceful life and does not think any more about the pleasure of an act without consequences, of a union without offspring. There are countless examples of the immense care animals take in raising their young. A mother guides her young while they are unable to fend for themselves; but once this goal is achieved, the young animal becomes an adult and "lives its own life", and the mother goes back to her old life. There is no sense of possession; there is simply a sense of motherhood and care, that ends when the natural cycle of the young comes to an end, once they have grown into an adult.

All animals know how to die, and they do so silently, serenely, some perhaps with a hint of sadness, but without despair. Animals don't think... and perhaps that's why they don't question their own eternity. They accept their cycles and live them without thinking about them rationally. They "feel" life rather than rationalizing it. That is why we don't see in them the typical psychological fatigue that is so fatal to humans.

***

In animals, there are two types of intelligence: one arises out of their own instinctive development and causes them to act in the appropriate way at each stage of their lives, and makes them "wise" in their own field from birth. The other is like a "borrowed" intelligence, which is higher than that of the species itself; a kind of "group soul" which causes them to behave in ultra-intelligent ways that are astonishing to us.

In the game of Maya, everything is perfectly interconnected. Stones, in their world of unmoving matter, have a foretaste of the movement that will one day develop in them as they expand and contract. Plants, in their vitality rooted in the earth, have a foretaste of feelings when they flourish better or worse depending on how they are treated. And animals, in their world of emotions, have a foretaste of the intelligence that time will bring them in the future. We will also see how rational human beings have reflections of supra-rational stages, which for now are not yet fully part of us but will one day be ours through the process of constant evolution.

We can see numerous examples of higher intelligence in animals. Enough has already been said and written about the lives of ants and bees. It is astonishing to observe the formations of birds in flight, and the migratory instinct that takes them from one part of the globe to another.

Animals have an intelligence that enables them to deal with new situations, overcome obstacles, heal wounds, recognize their land and travel along almost unknown paths. There is a kind of "radar" within them that comes to them from beyond their world of healthy instincts and pure emotions; a radar which is the archetype of the mind, a form of practical, unobstructed intelligence, slightly different from that which humans currently possess. It could be referred to as the "group soul", as mentioned above, or the "great mind of the animal world".

***

But, as emotions are the most outstanding elements in the animal world, we want to devote a little attention to them, so that we can see them separately from the games of Maya.

Animals are not all the same; just as with humans, plants and stones, some are more evolved than others. We tend to accept that the most evolved ones are those we recognize as domesticated. These live with humans, accept and share their laws, respect them and love them.

The word "loyalty" is hardly sufficient to express what I truly mean with regard to domestic animals. There is indeed loyalty; to some extent, the best examples of loyalty – to our shame – are to be found in animals.

But I think that animals "worship" humans because they are like gods for them. The plant is a god to the stone, and the animal is, in a way, a god to the plant. Thus, the human being is the god of the animals, the perfect being to whom, over the centuries, they will be able to become more and more similar.

The domestic animal loves its gods, and when it finds "its god", its master, even the word love falls short. It is an unconditional, undemanding love, without resentment. It is simply love.

Have you seen how these animals always seek the company of their masters?

Have you seen how they defend them, how they follow them even beyond the grave? Have you seen how they worship their clothes, their smell, their voice, everything about them? How they adopt a state of attention at just a word from the master?

Although Maya plays with us and our senses, although our intelligence is still in the process of being structured, there is a very important lesson to be learned here.

We still have a long way to go before we can be considered "domesticated human beings", evolved human beings. We do not recognize our gods as readily as animals do. And even if these gods were to show themselves to us, we would neither love nor obey them; divine laws are mere abstractions and the sacredness of keeping one's word is a mere convention in most cases. We know nothing of true devotion and true loyalty. And if we had to choose between remaining among the living or following our gods into death... our human selfishness and the “advantages of the mind” would lead us to choose the wrong path.

In the midst of the illusion that envelops us, I have just glimpsed a glimmer of truth: if animals are pure and healthy in their instincts, their emotions and their basic intelligence, should we not think about their pure love for God? Why not let ourselves be guided by this instinct of theirs, which infallibly seeks what is higher than themselves? If we did so, perhaps our human mind might finally be useful for something.

MAN

Man is, perhaps, the creature who is most trapped by the games of Maya.

This is because, after climbing the ladder of evolution, there is something in us of stone, something of plant, something of animal and something that defines us as human beings. From the stones we have our body, whose material constitution is no different from that of rocks and earth. From plants we have the possibility of life and growth. With animals we share the world of the senses. And the reasoning capacity is what marks us out as distinctly human, although that part of us – the mind – does not yet have the perfection of the body, the vitality or the emotions; the mind is halfway through its development; the mind is young, weak in many respects and can be easily deceived, falling readily into the nets of illusion.

Thus, human beings have the advantages and the problems of the three worlds that have preceded us on the ladder of life. And among all these problems is the fact that we now have a threefold possibility of falling into the game of Maya, plus our own particular possibility, which is the mind. We fall like stones, like plants, like animals and as human beings properly speaking.

***

But what we share with the known kingdoms of Nature is not the only thing that makes us the playthings of illusion. A decisive element in this matter is the precariousness of the human condition.

Let us imagine a man who tries to climb a mountain and, when he is halfway up, begins to lose his balance; it will cost him the same amount of effort to go up as to go down, because the distance he has come and the distance that still lies before him are the same. But his feet tremble as they seek in vain for some support, and his hands are torn as they try desperately to hold onto anything solid. Man is trapped between his feet which no longer support him and his hands which are almost incapable of helping him to climb upwards. He is crucified in space: with his feet on an earth and his arms in a sky which do not help him to transcend the false equilibrium of the intervening space.

But the easiest thing, in the example of our trapped man, is to fall rather than to keep climbing upwards.

The part of the mountain already climbed is comparable to the evolution that human beings have already achieved, all their accumulated experiences as a stone, a plant, an animal and even as a human being. The part still to be climbed is what remains on the path of evolution. If we identify the part already climbed with material experience, and the part still to be climbed with spiritual experience, we will see clearly why it is easier to fall than to climb. The force of gravity of matter is greater for this intermediate human being than the force of attraction of the spirit.

From this mid-point – even if it is not a point of balance – man feels more closely connected with his material condition of rock, tree or beast than with his divine future as a spiritualized being. Although he longs to evolve, to attain it requires a lot of hard work. Even if he wants to be better, he is afraid to leave behind everything that has represented his life until that moment. In his blindness brought about by Maya, he wants to be a god without ceasing to be a human being.

It is as if the stone wanted to be a plant, but without having to free itself from the inert heaviness of its body. Or as if the tree wanted to be an animal, but without detaching itself from its roots in the earth.

The resolution of this situation of precarious equilibrium inevitably involves a sacrifice for the human being. In order to climb what remains of the mountain and to be able to use our hands freely, we will need to throw away all superfluous elements; any extra baggage is too much when we are climbing upwards. What was a staff on one part of the path becomes a heavy burden at the next stage. In order to be a human being, one cannot behave like a stone, a plant or an animal; those are things from the past which can be used in the present, but which must not control us in the present. In order to be a superman, one has to cease to be a man; in order to obey the ancestral command of the soul, to heed that call which comes from far away and obliges us to take another step, we have to abandon the false equilibrium of the cross in space. In a word: we have to make a decision, we have to make a choice.

***

That is why Maya plays with human beings, with those who are eternally indecisive, and in order to have a more enjoyable game, she increases the sensation of instability more and more, pretending that the threads of this net of fantastic illusion are planks of salvation, though they are no more durable than the spiders' threads that they actually are.

That is why Maya plays with our senses and with our young minds, making us see what does not exist.

The senses deceive us, not because they are not working well, but because we give too much value to what they show us. Touch, hearing, sight, taste and smell are useful for measuring particular elements in the world around us, and for transmitting them to our consciousness. But if we add to the simple transmission of the measurements of the senses the passion of the feelings, like or dislike, excessive reasoning about what is valuable and what is not; then the senses, become distorted and the image that reaches our mind is devoid of reality. It is just another illusion which Maya has taken an active part in creating. We no longer see a colour: we see something that we like or dislike; we no longer hear a sound, but we calculate the wavelength.

Which parts of us are mainly responsible for interfering with the proper functioning of the senses? The emotions and the mind. Or, to put it more simply: the mind that we humans currently work with, which, far from being pure, is tainted with selfish emotions. With great wisdom, the ancient sages used to say that the mind is the king of the senses. In its human "superiority", it tries to rule over all that lies within its reach in the sphere of life. But this mind is the mind of precarious equilibrium, that which has not yet entirely forgotten its animal stage – which is why it is full of passions – and which finds it hard to glimpse its higher future. It rules egoistically: it appears to have a master who is our self, and it flatters us with its egoism; but in truth, it serves Maya, purely and exclusively.

***

The list of traps into which human beings can fall is a long one. And the traps become more and more dangerous as the senses and the mind confuse our vision.

Our body is no longer as simple as a rock. It has demands that exceed its size and its possibilities of action; but passion infuses life into those bodies, which become worn out by the efforts and perish before their time, and not in a good way. People don't eat, sleep, drink or love "like animals", but much worse.

The natural vitality of our bodies is exacerbated and, far from being happy like plants, we rush about, choking ourselves in smoke, sweating and going round and round in a meaningless way, neglecting the health which we will only come to regret once we have lost it.

As for the emotions, they dominate us to such an extent that they create a real fog around us. When they grow and multiply, when they become obsessive and turn into passions, it becomes impossible to act like a human being: it becomes impossible to think, to reason, to analyze, to weigh up and decide. Passion demands everything, and also destroys everything, turning our own forces against us.

The mind believes that it thinks, but the inertia of the material world, in which it has become trapped, makes its heavy and apathetic. The mind lets itself be thought. It lets itself be won over by opinions, prefabricated ideas and fashions, until it becomes completely paralyzed. It then becomes like a rusty old watch whose hands can no longer move, although there will always be some gullible person who, taken in by its outer appearance, claims that it is a watch. But what is the use of a watch that doesn't tell the time? And what is the use of a mind that has lost the simple ability to observe, compare, know and discern?

***

Deep within this human being who is trapped by illusion, there is a weak little creature who softly moans. It is even younger than the young mind which has become vain and proud of its power. It is the spark of spirit, which is trying to make itself heard. It is the ancestral voice demanding the fulfilment of a destiny. It is reality, which is attempting to remove the veil of Maya from the eyes that cannot see. It is the weak spark of spirit which nevertheless, as long as it remains alight, has hidden powers to grow and become more powerful than all the false powers. It is the weak sound that will become the roar of a storm. "It is the trickle that presages the torrent..." It is Man.

NATURE

There is nothing that seems so natural to the human being as Nature. Not natural in the philosophical sense of the word, in the sense of everything responding to an ordered plan of evolution and divine law. But natural in the human sense, in other words, of everything being at the service of the human being: the idea that everything exists simply to benefit human beings, or for human beings to extract benefit from things.

All the kingdoms that are less developed than the human and coexist with us within the shared framework of Nature are at our disposal. Stones can be used without a second thought; plants are good for eating or for making things; animals are eaten – naturally – or are made use of for many different tasks. The earth is there so that the seeds we plant in it may germinate, or to provide us with its hidden treasures as quickly and easily as possible. And I have even heard it said that the stars in the sky are lanterns that God has placed there to guide man on his nocturnal wanderings; if the latter is poetry, then it is very beautiful. But if it is utilitarianism – as I rather fear it is – then we must conclude that the stars have no other choice but to shine and give light, because human beings – MAN in the generic sense – the most "perfect" being in creation – cannot see well at night.

It is when we see things through this tinted lens that we fall into the traps of the game of Maya and, instead of learning from the open book that Nature represents, we ruthlessly deface its pages and its covers, in this case without any real benefit.

Nature is the natural stage on which we can undergo the experiences we need in this phase of our existence. And it is not only we humans, but also stones, plants, animals and heavenly bodies, that are alive and experience and express themselves in this world. The human being is simply one of the many rungs that make up the great ladder of evolution. And who knows whether or not there are other beings in Nature who are higher than human beings and whom we are unable to see? Because if we can see so many things, why should we not be able to see what is directly above us?

But matter adopts multiple – almost infinite – forms of manifestation. Some are concrete and visible, others are less so and pass us by unseen. When the sun floods the sky with its blinding light, would we say that the stars do not exist? And when the night covers our surroundings with serene darkness, and the stars begin to shine, would we say that colours do not exist? There are moments when some things are seen and others are not. There are moments when some things are manifested and others are not. But all things are alive. Yes, it depends on the moments, but also on our capacity for observation, understanding and even evolution, as to whether we are aware of them or not.

It is not enough to see in order to understand. The lack of

understanding and wisdom reduces vision enormously. For one for whom life is a question of material subsistence, Nature is silent. For one for whom inner awakening has begun to manifest, Nature is – as we were saying before and so many others have said – an open book that presents an infinite source of knowledge. A leaf, seen with indifference, says nothing; but it has a lot to teach us if we look at it carefully: then, a thousand and one intelligent details will appear, that tell us clearly about the life of that leaf. The colour, shape, veins, the way it receives air and sunlight – all are vital aspects and indicators of the intelligence that governs that vitality.

In the same way, it is likely that we who are blinded by Maya do not see life-forms that are higher than our own, simply because we are looking at Nature with the indifference of an ignorant person. We just need to shake off a little of our drowsiness in order to understand.

Just as the future movement of the tree is alive in the stone; just as the future sensitivity of the animal is alive in plants; just as the future intelligence of the human being is alive in the animal, so the future spiritual wisdom of the superman is alive in man. We just have to shake off a little of our drowsiness for the future to resonate within us. We just have to open our eyes a little to notice that the human being, weighed down with so many imperfections, cannot be the ultimate and most perfect model of Nature. We just have to want it in order to understand that, if we can see glimpses of the future within us, that future may already exist somewhere, materialized in some form, in some dimension, in some key of our own Nature which, for the moment, eludes us.

***

Heaven and earth are the stages of Nature. In between them are expressed the infinite forms of life. From the heavens, they draw the cosmic force of the sidereal mystery, the mystery of the future. On the earth, they sink their roots into the other mystery, of the past: formation of matter. We have within us all the forms of life – as Plato said – a little of one thing and a little of the other, a little of matter and a little of spirit; and we carry within us, as we struggle upwards, the drama of trying to achieve the appropriate balance between one part and another.

All life forms – including ourselves as human beings – have a mother and a father. The mother is the horizontal earth, generous and giving of food, capable of sheltering us and sacrificing herself silently to satisfy our needs. The father is the vertical sky, who calls us upwards, obliging us to lift up our eyes, who does not protect us, but demands sacrifices of us, who does not give us easy things, but promises health-giving difficulties. Per aspera ad astra: through difficulties to the stars.

***

Everything in Nature vibrates and sings. Nothing stands still. Everything is going somewhere, everything fulfils its own destiny.

That is why Pythagoras spoke about the "music of the spheres", the movement of the planets and stars and the symphony they create through the revolutions of their celestial bodies.

Our terrestrial Nature also vibrates and sings. It also

produces special sounds that make up the rhythm of its own movement. Have you ever stood in absolute silence, listening only to the murmur of Nature? Not the nature imagined by human beings, not the noise of the big cities, not the noise of machines. Have you ever heard the natural sound of the wind, of the leaves in the trees, of the waves on the sea, of the thousands of tiny little animals teeming almost unnoticed around us?

It is said by those who know, that our Nature, our Earth, sings the sound which we call 'F'. Our musical scale is based on seven sounds: C, D, E, F, G, A and B. Seven sounds that correspond to seven colours. Our sound, the sound of our Nature, which we are able to perceive, is the middle sound, like that of the human being crucified in space, with three sounds below it and three above, with one part of the path travelled and another part still to be travelled. The mixture of the one and the other. That is Nature. We just need to shake off a little of our drowsiness and we will hear it sing. It is alive; it is our source of material life; Maya protects herself within it, playing with it and with us. What could be more natural than this?

THE FOUR SEASONS

When scientists try to explain the reason for the changes in climate which periodically occur on our planet, they refer to the tilt of the Earth's axis in relation to the plane it describes in its rotation around the Sun. This, added to the fact that there are moments when the Earth is closer to the Sun or further away from it, means that there are different changes over the course of a year, which we classify into four groups and, traditionally, we call seasons.

However, when we play with Maya, it is not enough to see a phenomenon; Maya never does things just for the sake of it. The interesting thing is to know what was Maya's intention on the day when she changed the tilt of the Earth's axis.

Ancient traditions, which we find in all the high civilizations, say that there were past ages when the Earth's axis was not tilted, but was perfectly vertical. In those times, there was a central strip of land on the Earth which, because of its climatic conditions, might well have been what we usually describe as paradise: an eternal spring, a constant and pleasant temperature, when days were equal to nights, and it was enormously easy to sow and harvest almost without any effort.

At that time human beings were probably also different from

the way we are now. The same traditions tell us that those human beings were innocent, simple, not very intelligent or rational, and that they had not had so much experience and therefore did not have the shrewdness that naturally arises from it. These human beings were only concerned about surviving, and their only religion was a reverence for the immensity of Nature, which allowed them to have an intuition of God.

But things changed.

One day, after the catastrophe had come upon them – which is also recorded by ancient traditions – everything changed on the face of the planet, and the poles took a new direction. The earthly paradise had come to an end. The time of suffering, toil, the slow and painful acquisition of consciousness by human beings, had begun.

In this way, the seasons came into being, with their cyclic renewals. People came to know heat and cold, light and darkness, rain and drought, windy and calm days. Human beings had to fight hard to conquer this new Earth, and had to observe Nature patiently in order to learn which were the best times to undertake their work and gather its fruits. They also had to find shelter and somewhere to live, because there were long and freezing nights, and days of scorching sun. In this way, a series of extremely long migrations began, in which people followed the dream of finding a better place to settle down.

The Earth, that great mother who is so good at supporting so many diverse forms of life, once more offered her own change and sacrifice to provide a new lesson.

The human beings who came after the change were no longer so innocently ignorant as they had been before. In these new human beings a spark of consciousness had awakened, and for that spark to develop in a healthy way, they had to overcome a long series of trials.

Work, which lent value to their existence and gave them the feeling that the days of their lives were useful, was one of the trials.

And perhaps the most important trial of all was to experience, in themselves and in the whole of Nature around them, the rhythm of time evolving through the cycles.

***

If we had to apply one characteristic to the unfolding of the seasons in order to define them better, we could refer to a cycle that is repeated annually. No one is surprised that the seasons succeed one another according to an established rhythm and always in the same order. Spring, summer, autumn, winter. In fact, it would be surprising if it did not happen in that way.

Spring is the birth of life on the earth. It is the time when everything blossoms and opens itself to the beneficent rays of the sun. It is the awakening, the warm breath of life beginning to manifest itself.

Summer is the fullness of life. What had been hinted at in spring has now become a complete reality. It is the time of the ripe fruits.

In autumn, life begins gently to decline; the leaves lose their brightness and can no longer remain attached to the branches; the flowers and fruits cease to exist. Golden colours replace green.

And winter is the death of Nature. Now everything sleeps and rests, although life continues in a latent form in the depths of the roots. It is the time of rest, though not a final rest. A new spring will emerge after the winter, and what had been asleep will open its eyes to life once more.

But these cycles that we accept so easily in Nature are enormously difficult to apply to human beings. The game of Maya seeks to make humans feel like a special creation within the whole, like something that does not have to obey the same laws that govern everything else. And these special, disobedient human beings are, in their consciousness, outside the system. They live the seasons externally, but they cannot feel them within themselves. They have not managed to conceive that their own lives are subject to a cycle that is very similar to that of the seasons.

Human beings are also born, develop, reach their fullness, decline and die. But their blindness prevents them from recognizing that their death is not final, just as no form of rest is final in Nature. They do not realize that they too will be reborn with the same simplicity as trees are reborn, when the time comes. They cannot hope to be reborn with the same body, just as the tree cannot demand to have the same leaves as the previous summer. New leaves, new bodies: the same roots, the same soul.

The cycles of time revolve in a circular manner, adding experiences which bring the rotation closer to the centre of the circle. The seasons revolve untiringly; and human beings evolve unconsciously, following with pain the game of Maya of their own death, until they attain the consciousness of their immortality.

DAY AND NIGHT

These constitute another kind of cycle, even if they are repeated in the brief time that we humans count as 24 hours. This cycle generates much less fear than the other great cycle of the seasons. We observe it more frequently and, even though our memory is weak, it can remember from one day to another, from one night to another. That possibility of memory takes away fear.

Day and night are associated with the activity and rest of living beings. Although all living beings are subject to tiredness and we have to combine work with rest, it is good that Nature reminds us of this fact when she herself assumes external forms that incline us towards one or the other.

Day begins when the Sun appears, and this is an invitation to a wide variety of tasks. The stone expands; the plant begins its process of photosynthesis; animals emit their peculiar sounds and emerge in search of their daily sustenance. And we human beings do whatever we can, although the main thing is the sensation that we have to do something while the Sun is shining.

Night begins when the Sun disappears from view. Then the stone contracts, leaves curl up, animals become silent and seek refuge in their dens or nests; and human beings also feel overcome by the need for rest and sleep.

***

This is another of the games of Maya; it is a merciful illusion, since our day and our night are not absolute values; while I have light, there are parts of the Earth that are in darkness; and when it is night for me, the Sun will be shining somewhere else. But this illusion helps us to maintain our vital rhythm.

Human beings are so disordered that, without the guidance of day and night, they would fall into one of the two extremes: either absolute apathy or unrestrained activity. In human beings who are blinded by Maya, the law of passion overcomes the law of activity: this is how passion leads us into excessive action or inaction, without considering the equilibrium of the middle way.

In spite of everything, just as Nature does not always manage to impact the mind of human beings and make them understand the mysterious rhythm of the seasons, it is not absolutely successful either when it tries to imprint on them the rhythm of action and rest.

In human beings who are dominated by the passion of apathy, life is a perpetual "night", which does not mean that there is absolute inactivity, because that is impossible, but that there is a lack of good activity, an activity that creates and produces. Instead, the lack of useful occupations gives rise to an exacerbated development of instincts and base emotions, spending all the hours of the day imagining new enjoyments and emotional pleasures... as long as they don't require too much effort.

This psychological "night" is very similar to death; the consciousness remains as asleep as if we had never appeared in life. And Maya is not interested in human beings dying too soon; one or another of its needles will come to prick the apathetic person and take him out of his lethargy.

In human beings who are dominated by the passion of ceaseless activity, pride is the ally of action, and they see it as cowardly or stupid to stop for a single instant in the mad race of life, even if they don't always know exactly what they are doing, for what purpose or why. This activity without rest, that of the perpetual "day", ends by destroying the physical, psychological and mental forces of the individual, that is to say, it is another way of leading him to death. And Maya is not interested in us dying too soon.

The cycle of day and night thus becomes an energy that guides us to move and to stop moving, in accordance with the general plan of the whole of which we are a part.

The power of example is a great teacher; Maya makes use of that power. What Nature does, we all do, or at least we feel a great need to do it, and a great uneasiness when we don't do it.

***

Depending on the different human natures, some people appreciate the day more, and others the night.

Those who love the day and the light of the Sun defend the vivifying brightness that gives colour and warmth to things.

They bless the possibility of seeing, admiring and enjoying the landscape, sound, the clarity of forms.

Those who love the night and the light of the Moon are grateful for that cloak of merciful darkness that makes all things beautiful, and that tenuous, silvery radiance that creates mysterious shadows and vague murmurs that match the rhythm of our steps. Although it is true that the Sun is no longer shining, we can, on the other hand, see the stars, which would be hidden during the day.

The day and the Sun are the exaltation of manifested life, the worship of the mystery of creation, expressed in its greatest beauty. Night and the stars are the representation of the other cosmic and infinite mystery, reflected in a sky filled with distant worlds that make us feel small in the face of immensity. During the day we see the Earth and ourselves better, and this is necessary. During the night, darkness prevents us from seeing things close up, but allows us to look up at sidereal space; and that is also necessary.

That is why Maya plays with the cycles. That is why it is so difficult to choose. That is why it is so difficult not to be biased when one is trying to be part of this revolving wheel, which invites us successively to sleep and to wake, depending on the relative position of its spokes.

If we draw back the veils and learn to see this little cycle of sleep and waking, we will be able to make a leap to the great dimension of the other cycle of life and death.

THE EARTH

The Earth is a living being, although the games of Maya make it appear to human beings as no more than the container or habitat where our existence runs its course. In this way, the Earth has no more importance for many people than a set of bricks that are well fitted together, and there are even some, entirely blinded by illusion, who cannot imagine how we humans were not the builders of something as "simple" as the Earth.

However, the Earth is alive and, among its many mysteries is that of giving us shelter on its surface, and enduring – because no other expression would be appropriate – the use and abuse we make of it and its properties. Just as our human body carries within it thousands of infinitesimal lives of which we are not even aware, so the Earth also carries us upon itself, and the fact that those who are carried are alive does not mean that the carrier is not also alive.

***

Like all living beings, the Earth has a soul and a body. Of its soul there is little we can say, since if we barely know anything about our own, it will be difficult for us to know anything about another's. To judge by what Plato taught, we can deduce something about the soul of the Earth, from the moment when it manifests in an almost spherical body. Plato said that the sphere is the most perfect of geometric bodies and that living forms tend towards the sphere as they become more and more perfect.

We can say something, on the other hand, about the body of the Earth, because there are many things that can be glimpsed between the veils of Maya.

Its large body – in comparison to our own – has, in its own proportions, the same characteristics as the human being: it is born, grows and dies. In the meantime, as long as it is alive, it can suffer illnesses, change position, feel well, sleep or be awake. In this way, we can have a better understanding of many phenomena which, when explained only through the lens of science, appear cold and unintelligible.

Thus, there is the possibility of finding a logical explanation for the many traditions that exist about great floods, terrifying glaciations and phenomenal ice melts. Let us suppose that the Earth falls ill and, in order to cure its fevers, it covers itself with ice to refresh itself; it sleeps and rests under the cold layer which it can produce by the power of its own will, until the illness has subsided. Then, the ice begins to melt, the floods come... Human beings, disconnected from the process of the planet, only experience the dramas of these great cataclysms and record them through long-lasting myths which contain deep meanings.

Let us suppose that, like every living being, the Earth sometimes has a need to change position. Although the movement of these large bodies is more disciplined than it is in human beings, however slight that movement is, it would be widely felt by the other living beings living on them. And this explains those other traditions that remind us of the change undergone by the Earth's axis, not on one, but several occasions, when it moved from a vertical position to another more tilted position, as it is in the current age.

Let us think of the Earth as a being that ages; thus, when it was young, its temperature was mild and warm; but as it grows older it slowly becomes colder, as if the life was withdrawing from it. And this would help us understand something about the changes of temperature that are beginning to be recorded by scientists, or the small micro-glaciations that succeed one another, as if the Earth were taking a nap from time to time, as a result of which its vital heat would be reduced.

There is life on Earth because life germinates within it. The Earth is good for human beings, for animals, for plants. It generates in its depths the most varied and wonderful precious stones, and produces within its hidden interior bewildering geological changes, giving rise to carbon compounds or diamonds, the mortal remains of ancient animals or petroleum. Who has been able to explain the marvel of the Earth's components, perfectly adapted and transformed over time into the physical bodies of animals and human beings? If we believe that our body is alive, we cannot fail to accept the life of the Earth, since there is nothing in our bodies that does not come from it. Could something living be formed out of something that is inert?

***

Sometimes, the veil of Maya makes it difficult to see things clearly, and it is not easy to perceive the similarities between the life of the Earth and that of human beings. But things are "as above, so below", as the famous ancient Hermetic aphorism states.

The Earth also has a system of irrigation and respiration. For us, its seas, the course of its rivers, the currents of air that circulate within the planet, forming gases which, on occasions, emerge through the mouths of volcanoes, continue to be a mystery. For us, the tireless psyche of the planet, which never falters and inexorably continues to carry out its functions, continues to be a mystery. If only we too could achieve that continuity, that profound sense of duty, without ever tiring, without our enthusiasm ever running out. For us, the intelligence of the Earth continues to be a mystery and, on more than one occasion, has confounded the laws of scientists, changing its rhythms, accelerating or slowing down its processes, and even changing the direction of its orbit in order to avoid a collision with a comet.

***

Of all its mysteries, the Earth does offer us a little knowledge of its surface. We know little or nothing of what exists in its interior; we can dream, we can "journey to the centre of the Earth", but in truth, Maya only lets us know about the earth on which we stand.

The planet has always been thought of, not in terms of itself as a whole, but in terms of the part of the whole that we use. Most of the planet is made up of water; dry land is a lesser portion, but it is the one that we are interested in, because we live on it; we travel the seas, but it is on dry land that we live.

Support, settlement, a secure base: that is the symbol of Earth because of its main constituent. That is the symbol of the matter that supports us. When the alchemists of old equated earth with matter, they did so not in the pejorative sense of that which is coarse and of the senses. Matter is the sustaining fabric, which can support and carry other more subtle principles. Thus, the Earth supports us, and we know that on it we can feel firm. It is matter, our matter, the matter of which we are formed and constituted, and which bears us. It is skin and bone. It is the ground on which we rest and the ground of mysteries; we can put our hands into it – our hands of earth – as the trees put their roots into it. Strange metals and sparkling stones emerge from it, and in deep caves are hidden the waters and winds of ancient works which little spirits forged long ago.

***

The Earth is beautiful. In it there is a principle of harmony that characterizes all living beings alike, whatever their size. In it there is an equilibrium that speaks to us of the hand of God, or the "digits of God", as the classical Greeks used to say. Its colours are wonderfully mixed, giving rise to a symphony of different shades, as a challenge to the imagination of the most fervent of artists. Rocks assume strange contours. Gems organize themselves according to geometric patterns. And from time to time, some cave may open before the curiosity of man, to show that even within its body, the fingers of God have placed beauty in the Earth.

And Maya has clothed with threads of illusion this sphere that revolves rhythmically in space, holding us all together – the Earth and ourselves – in this great game of Life.

WATER

This is as fundamental an element on our planet as the solid part which we call earth. Even more: there is a greater proportion of liquid matter than solid matter on the Earth, and there is no solid part which is not in some way suffused or interpenetrated with liquid, or needs to be.

The prototype of the watery element is, for us, the sea. The sea is like the blood of the planet, vital, salty, full of energy itself and at the same time a giver of strength. The sea somehow contains all the forms of water: the salt water of which it is made, the fresh water of the rivers that flow into it and the vertical rains that result from the rising of vapour and the falling of the drops of liquid.

That is why the ancients spoke of the sea as if it were blood, and they knew that its many salts were not a reason to think of it as a heavy, inert being, almost dense at the depths of the ocean floor. They knew about this living blood, which carries different currents within it – cold or warm, flowing in one direction or another, so that that enormous liquid mass would never be at rest, constantly distributing its rich flow of energy – just as the blood circulates through channels in the body, depending largely on the currents of temperature.

***

Into this enormous source of aquatic life which is the sea, the veins of the rivers flow. They collect their material as they travel across the earth, between lakes and mountains, forests and deserts, and always, always, their current leads them to the sea.

What is the extraordinary game of Maya that causes these rivers always to end their journey in the sea? What is the force, the intelligence that animates them, so that they never lose their way? Here, Maya has taken great pains over its action, and there is no trickle of water, anywhere on the planet, that does not find a way to reach a greater source, which, in turn, will flow out into another and another, until finally reaching the infinite sea.

The fact is that water looks for water, by affinity; all this is part of the game of Maya. But the waters also have their own level of evolution, and they know that the tiniest drop has the same essence as that of the greatest of oceans. In this way, the little drop looks for its god, its goal of perfection, and longs to reach its ocean. The drop of fresh water, which is a child of the Earth, eventually needs to become the salty drop, which is the child of the sky. When it is small and separate, it has little value; when it merges with the sea, far from losing its personality as a little drop, it takes on the grandeur of the ocean.

That is why rivers, springs and streams always go to die – or to live? – in the sea.

***

Maya enjoys playing with the waters. Maya – and this is a secret which she does not tell very often – is also of a watery nature. Maya plays with the rivers, making them look like arms filled with life. She neatly touches up their banks, or leaves them isolated and flat in the midst of deserts. Sometimes, the riverbanks merge gently with the land; sometimes a ravine marks the division between one element and the other.

Maya plays with the rains. Have you ever seen how the wind makes raindrops fall at an angle? Have you ever noticed that sometimes, on the other hand, the stream of rain is completely straight and vertical? Have you ever seen how the drops change, sometimes being large and full, and at other times fine and soft? When the air and the wind change the appearance of the rain, it is Maya becoming merged with the air and the wind.

Maya plays with the sea. When Maya is wind, she ripples the salty surface and sketches on it curious forms of white foam. From the white foam, Maya caused Aphrodite to be born. When Maya is the Moon, she attracts the waters to her, and the sea rises up in search of that mirror in the sky which looks so much like it. When Maya is the sky, she plays with the sea to paint her best colours on it: the sea is sometimes blue, sometimes green, on some afternoons it is grey, violet before storms, black during the night.

***

The waters are the very image of movement. The clouds never cease to form and, once formed, never cease to fall. Rivers have a fixed goal and no one can divert them from their purpose. The sea is a mass which is never at rest, with or without waves, but always directing its movements towards its counterpart, earth. The sea learnt to play with Maya, and plays with the earth by eating away at its shores: it hides them from view and reveals them again, covers them and then leaves them alone, rises and falls, comes and goes. This sea and this land are like children who, though different in their appearances, share the same essence, and have learnt the same game based on the same illusion: how can I manage to merge with you? The sea says this to the land, and the sands say it to the sea.

***

It is true that the solid earth contains infinite forms of life. But how many forms live in the sea? Stones, plants and animals have found ways of adapting to the liquid element, and there they have developed a great variety of appearances, as beautiful and harmonious as the fingers of Maya, which have given them their colour.

Algae and corals, stones and giant ferns, share their existence with a rich variety of fishes, as if all these life-forms were the work of a very definite digit of the hand of God.

The same game of Nature takes place in the interior world of water. There is a certain cruelty – from the viewpoint of human beings – which, from the viewpoint of Nature, is simply the law of material life. All this is the basis for the often repeated, but little understood saying that "the big fish eats the little fish". The small drop longs to be the size of the sea. The little fish is food for the big fish. The flying insect is trapped by a bird. Everything small gravitates towards the supreme; and the supreme attracts the small, to eat it, to look after it, to make it bigger, to seat it on the throne next to itself.

***

The sea, this child whom we saw before playing with the land, can sometimes take on a terrifying aspect, ceasing to be the innocent infant and becoming a monster that swallows and destroys everything. The raging sea is the unleashed force of life that nothing can withstand.

On more than one occasion, the sea has thrown its claws onto the land; not only did it kiss the shores and flirt with the sands, but it swallowed entire cities, with their human inhabitants and their hopes, their successes and their mistakes. And now, the sea stores in its depths hidden mysteries which we human beings of the present cannot – and sometimes do not want to – remember. Ruins of past worlds, continents that no longer exist, roads along which nobody travels, ships that will never float again, bodies that have become merged with the salt of the sea... It is the ever active life of the waters, which destroys the cyclical life of the earth: life devouring life, as the big fish devours the little one.

***

If the solid earth is the symbol of a base and support, water – the sea – is the symbol of vitality. It is the life of the body and it is also the prototype of spiritual life. When the waters flow horizontally, over the earth, parallel to the earth, it is corporeal life; when the waters fall vertically as rain, it is the spirit that descends and animates the empty corporeal shell. That is why the sea is both Mother and Father. It is the great mother who stores within herself the seed of all generation; it is the beginning of things, and perhaps the end. And it has from the spiritual father the possibility of rising up in subtle vapour to search in the sky for the indispensable essence that life needs in order to become Life.

Current of energy... Blood? Sea? Life...

AIR

It is much more subtle than earth and water and, as a result, it presents a much more fragile appearance. However, Maya is playing with our senses again: the air is more subtle, much more mobile than other forms of matter but, far from being weaker, it is much stronger and more powerful.

With our fingers of flesh, we cannot hold onto air. But it can pass through us, through the whole earth, and even through water, playing with all of us, enveloped in the magic of its subtle mobility. The less matter there is, the less resistance, the less weight; the more movement and force.

The whole Earth is permeated with air. The aerial element has the property of finding its way through the most unlikely cracks and openings. It filters down into the depths of the planet, causes strange internal whirlwinds which we never get to see and reaches the heart of fire, which sleeps in the deepest depths of the Earth; there it heats up and expands, and later comes out through other cracks and openings, but full of radiated energy, volcanic energy, in geysers that rise up in the midst of the sea, in fumes or vapours that emerge suddenly before the astonished eyes of human beings.

The air also plays on the surface of the Earth. It wanders

among the stones, singing with them mysterious songs, whose sounds we cannot write on a sheet of music. It hides among the foliage of plants and appears suddenly, like a naughty child, revealing its presence in the wonderful dance of leaves and shrubs, grasses and branches. It plays with human beings, messing up their clothes and hair and whispering its magic words in their ears. A never-ending dance, with quick or slow steps, either as a gentle breeze or an uncontrollable whirlwind, hiding in the midst of dizzying clouds of air. It raises particles of dust, blinds as it sweeps the roads, prepares for the arrival of rain.

Air and water are great friends, and they express this relationship in the most varied ways. There are days when their encounters can be seen in the gentle rippling of river currents, or in the tender waves of the sea as they reach the end of their race on the shore. It helps the waters to flow: it leads the rivers to the sea, and it leads the sea to its coasts; in this way, it shares in the constant movement that characterizes the whole of Nature. But there are days when water and air mingle passionately: winds and rains, waves and downpours, overflowing rivers, prodigious ocean storms, tell us of the tremendous force of that passion. It is then that the elements display all their power and terrify human beings, revealing the cosmic root from which they take their strength. If human beings knew how to look for their own roots, they would understand the water and the air of the storms, but as human beings are enclosed in their case of flesh, they are swept away and drowned by those other forces which, naturally, overwhelm them on the material level.

For the sages of antiquity, air was the symbol of the power of the psyche. Air was emotion, sentiments, passion, the changing mobility of the affective sphere. In order to understand it, we just need to play a little with the air and see it behind the veils of the wind.

The gentle breezes remind us of the calm and affectionate feelings that fill human beings when they are at peace, just as the breezes do with earthly Nature. The soft whispers which barely move the sands, which barely rouse the surface of the sea, or which gracefully move the green leaves of the trees, are very similar to the gentle words of affection which, from time to time, we humans know how to utter.

The tempestuous and furious winds are the very image of uncontrolled passions. They roar and attack, just as the passions shriek and destroy our psychological calm. Faced with the great storms of wind, which presage the no less great storms of water – we tend to hide to protect ourselves. Before the great outbursts of passion, we hardly have any defence. What safer refuge could we find than by learning to live a little higher up, on firmer ground?

If we understand that a storm sweeps away everything it encounters in its path, why have we not managed to see that violent and unrestrained desires can sweep away our own being? Why do we have faith in Nature and wait for the storm to pass, knowing that "nothing lasts forever"? And why, on the other hand, do we not have faith in ourselves, and fall at the first assault of the emotional winds?

Great is the force of the air, which can overcome earth and water, which can overcome our body and our vitality.

***

But we have said many times before that the games of Maya are not random or uncontrolled. It is our knowledge that can be random or uncontrolled unless it is based on firm laws.

Maya produces breezes, winds and storms, she plays with the air, but she follows laws that know of beginnings and ends, that know the how, why and wherefore of things.

Let us take as an example the simple but often forgotten process of our respiration. Every time we breathe in, the air, with its special vitality, enters our bodies. The unconsciousness with which we go through our physical existence means that we do not interfere too much in this process and, as a result, everything carries on rhythmically and mathematically, according to the order the air follows in its higher manifestations.

The air enters: the energy of this living element enters. The air is distributed and follows the channels established for it, coordinating its action with the other sacred rhythm of the beating heart, just as the winds combine with the rains and the sea. The air distributes its precious load, collects the unusable waste products of our organism and re-emerges, warm, almost fiery, like volcanic fumes of mud and lava. The air has given its life and its purity so that we can live. And we continue to think that it is by chance that we have two openings in the nose.

***

The air is alive. It comes and goes carrying its life to every corner. It penetrates the earth and the sea. It finds its place in stones, plants, animals and human beings. It knows its laws and plays at abiding by them. It sings, enjoys, laughs and cries: it is gentle emotion, overwhelming passion and sublime sentiment.

The air knows about transmutations; it knows how to roar with tempestuous fury, and it knows of pleasurable murmurs. And it has learned to enter, too, into pipes and tubes of matter which human beings have made to capture its song.

It was for this reason that the ancient Greeks used to say that the construction of musical instruments was a gift from heaven, and they thanked Apollo for such a wonderful present. Still today we continue to make instruments: it is enough to blow into them and press on the keys for the air to answer our call and sing with the sounds of a flute, the warmth of an oboe or the earthiness of a trombone.

And we who can master so well the air in these pipes and tubes with keys and holes – how long will it take us to learn the same game and master the wind of our passions, which blows without any instrument to contain them?

FIRE

Of all the elements we have been referring to until now – earth, water and air – fire is the most subtle, and perhaps corresponds in Nature to the highest and most active force that we can imagine for the moment, if we accept with the ancient sages that none of our present methods of understanding provides us with a complete knowledge of the world we live in.

Why the highest? Why the most active? If we analyze the behaviour of fire, we will also understand the reason for its superiority over the other elements, although to do so we may have to sharpen our mind and try to go deeper into the symbolic meanings beyond material appearances.

The Earth moves on the basis of transformations which, although they do not alter its essence, do modify its appearance. Chemical and physical changes are continually at work in the heart of the planet and, in combination with water, air and fire itself, the Earth undergoes variations without changing its position in space.

Water displays greater mobility; for it, there are no secrets concerning horizontal movement; rivers and seas move, with greater or lesser force, and sweep their beds from one end to another, although always resting upon Mother Earth, the necessary support that allows them to flow. Only in the form of rain does water assume a vertical position, similar to the movement of vertical spiritualization, as we will see shortly.

And what about air? It flows horizontally and sometimes vertically, sweeping the surface of the Earth, but without needing to support itself completely upon it; it does not have its roots in the seafloors or riverbeds.

Fire only needs a point of support at its base, and after that all its movements are vertical, an eternal dance with aspirations to go higher, the most perfect simile of human spirituality, which looks for its God above, barely supporting itself on the body in which it has to express itself.

***

Maya has tied together the ends of its game in such an exquisite way that nothing is isolated or subject to chance. Everything is connected, and each thing exists insofar as it is part of the rest.

In this way, fire needs air, without which it would be impossible for it to express itself. It supports itself on the Earth and, when it touches it, it consumes it, just as it consumes oxygen. It dries up the waters, and can even burn in contact with water, if we remember the old secret of the Greeks – now lost – of the so-called "Greek fire", which had the ability to keep burning in the sea.

As a sign of its superiority, fire penetrates everything and consumes everything, not in a simple display of destruction, but in a much more arduous work of liberation.

The constant game of Maya has led us to believe that water is the enemy of fire and that it is the only element that can sometimes defeat its spirited nature. This is partly true, and if we draw back the veils of illusion, we can easily see why this is so.

If water is vitality, it is the mother of life if we think of it as matter, which is why we compared it to the power of the seas on the Earth and the blood in the body. If fire is vitality, it is the father of life if we think of it as spirit, which is why it is often compared to the flames that consume everything on the Earth, and to the mind, which is the first rung on the human ladder to understanding truth.

Thus, we are presented with the struggle between water and fire, each of them fighting for the supremacy of their particular form of life. As long as the scales of our present evolution are not entirely in balance; as long as doubt continues to diminish our ability to discern between the benefits of matter and spirit; as long as this war of opposites remains unresolved for the human being, it is possible that water may conquer fire, or that fire may overcome despite all odds.

***

In ancient civilizations, our ancestors always offered particular worship to the deities of fire. They saw in them symbols of the most ancient and profound mystery, the outer form of which they expressed as war and sacrifice. War – as we have already explained – not as destruction, but as liberation.

Sacrifice is the *sacrum officium*, the sacred ceremony where fire plays its part as a higher and holy symbol. This is the fire regulated by ritual, the fire that can burn as efficiently in the humblest bowl of clay, as in incense burners on altars or in votive lamps in temples. It is also the fire that burns and gives light within man: it is the sacred spark that sets him apart from all the other kingdoms of Nature. Once ignited, it will bring about the decisive war between the little self and the greater self, between the life of the body, which is water, and the life of the soul, which is fire.

Maya permitting, may each human being become responsible for their own war, and offer their forces in support of the only possible victor.

MOVEMENT

Everything vibrates. The whole universe is in movement.

Although we may sometimes believe, carried away by the illusion of Maya, that we can perceive stillness and lack of movement, everything that is manifested forms part of this law of action.

We have already seen that, by the skilful design of Maya, each level of Nature is subject to a particular form of movement. The Earth rotates around its own axis and orbits around the Sun within the galaxy; and it is affected by thousands of movements in its interior. Water, air and fire move in and on the Earth, running, blowing, burning... and they move in their special worlds of life, emotion and mind.

Stones move by resisting movement and, at the limits of their forces, by expanding and contracting. Plants move by growing; animals do so by feeling; and human beings display a type of action that combines the resistance of the stone, the growth of the plant, the emotionality of the animal and the reasoning capacity particular to man.

If we consider the superimposed and combined existence of all these worlds, we will see that when matter appears to be still, it doesn't imply a lack of movement. The fact that we may be calmly seated does not mean that we are not breathing, or that our blood is not circulating or that many other vital functions are not continuing to take place; nor does it mean that we are not continually experiencing emotions and thoughts. Where is the stillness? Where is the activity?

What is this movement that affects the whole universe?

It is, to put it simply, a lack of equilibrium. Every movement is no more than a search for the missing equilibrium. All living things move because they need that equilibrium, that absent harmony, the final destination where repose is not inertia, but the stabilized sum of all movements.

As we go in search of equilibrium, we living beings are in perpetual movement, trying out the most varied paths and offering to outside eyes the very image of instability, lack of direction, total disorder.

Things come and go, are born and die, appear and disappear, succeed or fail, carried along by an instinct which, although it may apparently take the wrong direction, knows with certainty what is the final goal. That is why we can talk about correct and incorrect movements; the former are those which bring us closer to the goal, while the latter are those which take us away from it through error.

Maya actively participates in this game, especially if the goals are directly beneficial to her, that is to say, if the ends are focused on the success and multiplication of material life.

Maya cannot play – and does not play – with things of the soul. Once we have started to play in life, Maya delights us with the feeling of satisfaction when we have correctly found one of her paths, and punishes us with the sensation of pain when we move away from the designated path because of ignorance. And Maya neither delights nor punishes, but simply blinds, when the daring man, having learnt about the paths of the earth, attempts to try out those other paths that will open the doors of the spirit to him. Then, it is not just about finding the true path, but finding it despite the veils of Maya.

But in either case, movement never ceases. If we have made a mistake, it is a good reason for new movements to lead us away from the mistake. And if we have been successful, movement will continue on the basis of new successes we need to achieve.

***

What we human beings call action is the direct expression of movement. Action is movement with purpose – like all movements – and is designed to align with that purpose; it is an intentional movement – like all movements – but is conscious of that intention.

When the body moves instinctively, it simply moves; but if it expresses movement consciously, understanding the reason behind it, then it acts. Action is, therefore, proper to the conscious human being and, on planes below or above the human being, it is proper to a thinking and intelligent root, whether we find it in animals or in the stars.

All forms of life, to a greater or lesser extent, participate in action. The stone acts with its dim spark of consciousness; the plant acts when it enters into contact with Nature and allows itself to be kissed by the water and the wind, or lets itself be caressed by human words of encouragement, or by the endearing chirping of birds. Animals act when they follow the laws of their species, when they hear the voice of survival, or when – once they have been domesticated – they recognize and follow the voice of a master.

Human beings also act when they finally manage to differentiate themselves from minerals, plants and animals. They do so when they allow their purely human gifts to prevail and when the consciousness knows that it is impossible to avoid action, since the whole universe is affected by this vibration of growth and search for equilibrium.

Two things must be understood, but without getting trapped in Maya's games. One is that nothing and no one can be released from their share of action; unconscious movement arises from existence itself, but action is what leads to greater degrees of evolution. If the whole world moves, someone who attempts not to move goes against the universal laws, which can only result in disaster. To remain motionless is not to stop acting: it is to act little and badly. Not to act is to ask others to fulfil our duties for us in the perfectly programmed machine of the cosmos; and this, as the ancient sacred books would say, is worse than being a thief.

The other thing that is required in action is also connected with traditional wisdom. Not all actions – even if they are conscious – have the same quality. The best action is right action, which is carried out without any intention of receiving a prize or a reward, although Maya makes sure that all actions that are carried out receive their due reward or punishment.

***

Conscious action is synonymous with commitment. All living beings – when they allow their inner principles to operate – are committed to life itself, to evolution, to destiny, to the consequences of everything that has been done. Action is commitment, and commitment is a higher form of consciousness: a consciousness that does not try to avoid its own responsibilities.

Conscious action is contrary to cowardice of any kind, because it implies commitment and the responsible acceptance of consequences. Cowards do not act: they “let things happen”, carried along by the dark forces of fear.

***

When primordial movement and action take objective form in the concrete world, we find the formula for work. It consists of many consecutive and related actions – whether these be material, psychological or mental – that lead to the achievement of an end in the most correct way possible.

Work is one of the ideal formulas for movement and, therefore, for achieving equilibrium. Whenever an object is well made, a task is completed or an objective is fulfilled, human beings can to some extent imagine the achievement of the final equilibrium towards which they are moving. It becomes an excellent incentive to strive for ever greater achievements and ever better results.

Is it not the same with Maya? Is she not also working when she plays?

FEELINGS

When the sphere of air manifests among human beings – and even among animals – it gives rise to the psyche and its characteristic expression: feelings. This is a wide-ranging world, where Maya perhaps feels more at home than anywhere else. Human beings are never so sensitive or so fallible, never so weak or so strong, never so great or so small and never so easy to convince as when they are involved in the game of the feelings.

Here everything is air: none of the solidity of the Earth on which we can support ourselves, and none of the rational depth of the fire of the mind in which we can justify ourselves. The feelings move, like the air, generally oscillating between the two dangerous extremes: pleasure and pain, like and dislike. And since their movement is pendular, they make us aware of suffering: when experiencing pleasure, we are afraid to lose it, and so we suffer; when experiencing pain, we have nothing but fallible sufferings in this sphere of the feelings: because whatever type of feeling is dominating us, we always tend to fall into pain.

What is necessary, then, is to find the ideal feeling, the middle way above the extremes: a feeling that goes beyond the duality of the game, that does not oscillate towards pleasure or pain, but sits on its pedestal and can watch the game of Maya, without taking part in it except in order to understand it.

***

Although they are all part of the same world, we can distinguish different qualities of feelings. There are some that are closer to perfection and others that are more coarse. Maya has taught us, through her games, that the best things are those that last longer. It is when we are guided by this teaching that we will recognize the best feelings from their ability to endure, and we will know we are dealing with ordinary feelings when they are no more than sparks that appear and as quickly disappear. Everything that lasts tends to escape the game of Maya; everything variable continues the game of manifested life in search of new experiences.

How do feelings come into being? In the first place, because there is a container, which is our psychological world, capable of giving them body and form. This world of the psyche reacts by creating feelings whenever an active agent sets them in motion. The whole of Nature takes part in this game, and when Maya dresses up in her most beautiful clothes, or when she tries to frighten us by displaying her ancestral force, the feelings open up before her.

Things attract us or repel us; everything enters our psyche through one of its two doors: like or dislike; and in this way we feel repelled by some beings and attracted by others. We live life by "feeling it" in this simple way, until we become capable of awakening to new and better systems of living.

Where do feelings come from? From other feelings. When

nature vibrates, Maya enters into action. Maya plays with objects of the senses. From the sensibility of Maya come our own feelings.

How do feelings grow, how do they keep themselves alive?

Entangled in the webs of Maya, we might believe that all emotions, whether positive or negative, are the product of chance; that they are born, live and die without following any law or established order. And so, we have grown accustomed to receiving them like someone who is watching the rain falling, and to feeling a vague nostalgia when we see them disappear, without knowing what to do to retain them or prolong them. Any kind of thought is therefore useless, because it is no more than an empty shell to contain a feeling which is no longer there.

However, feelings are not the product of chance. Just as they are born following certain rules, so they live and stay alive according to certain laws that are useful to know. To know these laws is to draw back the veil of Maya a little and to step aside from her game, which needs us to be fragile and insecure, changeable and suffering, so that we will accept everything she wants to impose on us.

If, on the physical plane, we have learnt that all objects require maintenance if they are to last, why should it not be the same with feelings? If we oil a machine, lubricate a car engine, clean furniture and clothes, why should feelings not be cleaned and "oiled"? If a body needs nourishment to prevent it from growing weak and falling ill, why should the feelings not also be nourished?

A feeling grows and stays alive as a result of great patience and effort. It is like a little plant whose roots must be cared for. What is the root of the feeling that we are nurturing? Once we have recognized it, knowing how it was born, we must water that original root daily so that the whole plant may live and thrive. But, we repeat, an enormous amount of constancy is needed: one cannot expect a feeling to live for no reason; this would be like believing that beings live for no reason, and that they die for no reason, governed only by absurd chance.

What is the best food for a good feeling? Just a few drops of tolerance... To know that the things that we love are not perfect, just as we are not perfect either. To accept these imperfections, not allowing them to destroy our feeling. But we should polish these imperfections little by little, starting with our own, and then continuing with the things we love.

***

Feelings remain pure when, as in all the orders of life, we don't allow them to become mixed. Just as no one would throw a sparkling diamond into the mud, we cannot afford the luxury of ruining our higher and relatively lasting feelings by covering them with the mud of doubts, resentment, ill will, anger or neglect. The good gardener removes the weeds that attack his plants; and those who have healthy feelings look after the jewels of their emotions as if they were their finest adornments.

The nobility of the feelings is a question of height: the closer we come to the crown of Maya, the nobler our feelings will be.

Nobility is lost when we fall, when our eyes look down at the feet of Maya, when instead of heaven we feed on earth. And feeling – as we said – is aerial: it fares better in the clouds than in the mud.

***

When feelings deviate from what they should be – when they become mixed, fall to lower levels, become debased, atrophy or grow gigantic like a cancer – we are in the presence of dangerous processes of denaturalization. Then Maya no longer plays with us; even she withdraws in horror at the obsessive terror of circular passions and progressive madness. Maya is capable of playing even with the veils of hate, but she finds no place for aberrations. Often, what we call "madness" is nothing but a total maladjustment to the great richness of nature, where everything has a place as long as we don't go outside its laws.

Here we can no longer refer to feelings: what was a delicate plant in the hands of a careful gardener is now a dry branch with thorns that injures anyone who touches it; a carnivorous flower that eats away at anything that comes close to it. It is uncontrolled passion, morbid desire, fixed and unbounded obsession, an uncontrolled gyratory movement that no longer finds its circle's centre.

***

Do feelings die? Certainly, like all living things, but how long they last depends on us. If we stop looking after our plant, which is a jewel, it will begin to decline before its time.

If we accept ourselves as we are, but demand of others – and everything in general – an absolute perfection, we have decreed the death of our feelings. If others have to understand us, but we don't have to understand them, we are incapable of feeling. If we only know how to ask for things, but do not understand about giving, there is no possible feeling.

Maya will then mercifully gather the torn remains of what once was and will keep them in a safe place until, after the necessary transmutations, they can be reborn and participate once again in the active game.

Has one of your feelings died? Don't be afraid: nothing dies. Everything is transformed. Even your psyche itself. From your apparent apathy, from your dry earth of winter, a new shoot of love or of hate will appear – and you will once more play with the precious stones of your feelings, even if you are unable to recognize them as such. This is also part of the game of Maya.

THOUGHT

This is a product of fire, a product of the human sphere, which crystallizes in the mind and in its particular form of action: thought. Through this action we can join things together and relate them to each other, as well as connecting with them ourselves.

There, in the depths of his being, where he does not often dwell, man feels alone and becomes aware of the overriding need to make contact with the things around him. But he does so like a child: he makes contact by attracting things towards him, trying to possess them, to touch them, to stare at them... The subtler threads of union that we can throw out towards the world and its objects are, precisely these mental threads, which operate like hooks that catch things and bring them closer to the self.

When we "think" of an object, we want to know it; to know it is to take hold of it and internalize it. But it is not easy to work with the mind, because its fiery nature makes it quick-moving, unstable and elusive; to hold on to a rock is not the same as to hold on to a thought and this is why, in the world of Maya, it is easier to define metals than to define those things that circulate through our mind. It is easier to tie things together with strings than with ideas; it is easier to approach a high mountain than one's own inner world.

***

The machinery of thought works with certain special units that we can call ideas. These come and go, and in the mental loom they weave their threads, seeking to possess more and more.

Ideas live in our mind, just as we humans live on the earth. They too come together in their moments of rest, when they don't have to work for the intellectual master who obliges them to stretch out and return within, continually bringing material for analysis. Then, ideas connect with each other by affinity, attracting similars and rejecting opposites. In this way, veritable families of ideas are born, becoming stronger as they grow in size and number.

This is why thought cannot always operate freely in its desire to know, since it has to face these group formations of ideas, which oblige it and impel it to know in a particular direction. Sometimes, we don't study what we want to know, but what our mental current and its associated ideas lead us to know.

This brings about a degeneration of thought: the process of "being thought". And the worst of it is that, in addition to "being thought" by our own mental families, we run the risk – always supported by the games of Maya – of "being thought" by the forces of Nature, by other human beings, by other superior and more organized minds than our own.

If we follow the forces of nature, we will be thought, but at least it will be in a healthy, natural way. If we follow other stronger and more positive minds, the risk is a benefit; but if these other minds are seeking to dominate the weak... then a sad fate awaits those who are thought. They will be left with nothing genuine and their life will be doomed to succumb to the interests of an enslaved mind.

That is why we can never give enough attention to the way in which our mind plays its games. We need to know the rules of this game and be able to intervene whenever thought is about to perish. If the law of ideas is to join together with others, let us try to join good, strong, positive ideas together; if we let bad ideas come together and then continue to relate to all the similar material that exists in the world outside us, we will have lost the condition of human beings, of thinking beings.

***

Despite the webs that Maya weaves around us, it is advisable to learn to distinguish the ideas that emerge authentically in ourselves – which don't need to be new, just new for us – from those other ideas that stick to us like the mud of the road we are travelling. If the mud dries and hardens, those borrowed, ready-made ideas will become encrusted in our minds and will do the same harm as any foreign body that is grafted onto its host; if the graft is accepted by our mental organism, all will be well, but if it is rejected, it will be like a veritable cancer of the mind.

Although it is true that Maya plays with matter and form, her game has winners, and the winners are the strong. A strong mind plays with ideas and wins, becoming the owner of what it possesses; a weak mind loses the game and is overcome by the invading ideas.

***

Just as we have learnt to create a good physical atmosphere to live in, so we must know that thought and the ideas with which it works, can forge an atmosphere as important and impactful as that which we achieve through good rooms, good furniture, good decoration, outer brightness and cleanliness.

If we agree that a group of beautiful objects contributes to a beautiful and harmonious atmosphere, we should know that a harmonious group of ideas also creates a favourable and pleasing atmosphere. This is true both for individuals and for human groups which come together and share common and beneficial elements. They are those places where you "have a good feeling" as soon as you enter, without being able to clearly explain why. In the same way, the accumulation of negative ideas generates an unpleasant aura that makes us want to get away as soon as possible. We can't explain what it is we dislike, but we know there is "something" in the atmosphere, something negative, bad, infectiously bad...

Today, when the world is committed to playing at ecological control – the cleaning of Nature – it should learn this other game that concerns not only bodies, but is able to clean something so much more important than physical matter: mental matter. Good food for the body and good food for ideas; this will give rise to a healthy human being.

How can we give good food to the mind? How can we support its health? By taking an old piece of advice from someone who knew a lot about how to escape from the nets of Maya: to think always in such a way that if someone were to ask us what we are thinking, we could say it aloud without being embarrassed.

***

Gliding high in the world of thought, above ordinary ideas, are the ideals, higher concepts that relate to elevated planes of being and states of humanity that seem perfect in comparison with the present ones. Now we are not just thinking about the problems of everyday life, with their habitual joys and sorrows; now what is important are the great questions of why, how, from where and to where? Our concern is now for all human beings and not just the small sphere of our individual life; we become interested in general solutions and not just in our own well-being.

These ideals are the great motors, the forces that encourage the good everyday ideas, right thought; they are the inspiration for the noblest feelings and the most just actions.

Then we can talk about human beings who, though they have not completely escaped from the games of Maya, understand the game, know its roots and know where the whole of life is going in its evolution. They are idealistic human beings; they have achieved a rare and marvellous miracle: they live and feel as they think.

INTUITION

In addition to rational thought, which works with ideas and shapes the mind, as we have said, there is in the human being another more subtle form of thought, which is intuition. The first form weaves threads in order to know: it is the reasoning faculty; the second grasps directly: it is intuition. We relate this second possibility of knowledge directly to intelligence.

Once again, Maya has changed the threads in her game and makes us believe that intelligence is a certain ability and skill that goes from the physical to the spiritual. To be "intelligent" is to be "smart", clever, with quick reactions, and in this way human beings eagerly work to develop intelligence as if it were a mental athletic competition.

Intelligence, however, is a gift that goes much deeper; it is more than thinking and reasoning; it is much more than responding rapidly to stimuli; it is to be able to understand life beyond the superficiality with which it presents itself to us. It is to recognize facts and make discerning judgements about them. Intelligence is to know how to choose and, even more importantly: to select one out of many other opportunities, to separate the good from the bad, the useful from the useless. All of that is intelligence, all of that is to work with intuition.

***

Intuition is to win the race against time. Old Chronos has been dominating us for many centuries, and has always imposed his condition: we human beings must develop ourselves on his terrain, and things must cost us... time. Acting takes time; feeling consumes our life; thinking uses up many hours; but by using our intuition... we break that barrier and grasp the essence of things in time, but without wasting time. Intuition is immediate understanding, which also contains the selective and decision-making capacity. What is understood – is it positive or negative? Will we be able to retain what we have understood or not? And if we can retain it, how will we use it to act? What do we choose to do and what do we do?

Someone who can use their intuition knows what they have, the value that is contained in what they have acquired, the possibilities of application this implies and the immediate way in which they will put it to use. In intuition there are no doubts, no unnecessary circumlocution: it is a race won against Chronos, beyond the veils with which Maya has attempted to cover up this reality.

***

Those who have never won this race against the discursive mind may believe that intuition is something like imagination. They may believe that what is "grasped" is actually "imagined". But – since it concerns the higher mind – if we spin a little more finely, we will be able to note that intuition is not to grasp what we want, or what we believe, or what we believe we are grasping; it is to grasp what Is.

Certainly, fantasy imagines things that don't exist, it goes into raptures in absurd games which not even Maya could make use of. But fantasy is totally different from intuition, because its images are sterile, they have no power to become real in the world of action.

Intuition, on the other hand, grasps realities, the few realities that the game of Maya allows us to glimpse; it treasures them and then converts them into successive descents which touch each of the planes of human expression in turn. And intuition can reach the mind in the form of an idea which, coloured with feelings and suitably vitalized, results in action. Intuition always results in appropriate action.

***

Intuition is to see with the eyes of the soul, but to act with the hands of the body. That is why we speak of intelligence: it is to know how to see and to know how to do. If it were just about seeing with the eyes of the body, those eyes would not see further than what our hands can do; that is why ability and skill are not the same as intelligence.

While the ordinary mind grasps things in a reduced and partial way, adapted to the thousand and one divisions of the interests of Maya; and while this mind can work quickly with the small parts that it cuts out of reality, the intuition enables us to have "sudden insights" that are less divided. Through the effects of intuition, it is possible to come a little closer to the elusive reality, to the amazing unity that hides behind the veils of Maya. We are no longer satisfied with the brief extracts that ordinary thought can digest, but we act through an organ that has the power to absorb more quantity, more wholeness. It is a step towards the unification of the forms of life, which is why we can speak about intuition as intelligence.

***

Maya prefers us to think, to waste our time bumbling along with our ideas while we play at living. Maya does not want us to discover her secret, her trap to force us to remain in the world. That is why she plays and makes us play, while at the same time leading us slowly away from the possibility of intuiting and grasping her truth.

Nevertheless, by watching Maya at play, by detaching ourselves a little and seeing ourselves participating unconsciously in that game of chess, a ray of intuition awakens. If we observe slowly the things around us and how our behaviour is affected by these things, a faint clarity begins to appear in the midst of our confusion and suddenly we understand a thousand reasons which mere reason cannot express.

Through her games, we are beginning to intuit the presence of Maya.

WILL

This is the force par excellence; it is the great burst of energy that sets the whole universe in motion. Not even Maya escapes the attractive power of will, since, at the command of the will, Maya develops her game.

This force is so infinite that it is applied on the most varied occasions. By the force of will, the stone remains intact without disintegrating, all the molecules of our body do not melt away and lose their form; and it is also the will that makes the heavenly bodies of our system revolve around a central Sun. The force is always the same, but the higher up it is applied, the subtler, the stronger and the more perfect it becomes.

This great force contains within itself the mystery of life; it is the life that appears in all beings. It manifests in the little insect that fights courageously for its existence, choosing a thousand rough paths and detours to escape the unconscious destruction we could inflict on it with just a finger. It can be heard in the little cat meowing sadly as it tries to run away from the death that is stalking it. We see it in the drop of water which tries to reach the ocean, and in the tiny little plant that peeps out desperately between two stones on the path shouting out its green right to life. The same vital force makes the star burst into a thousand lights before disappearing, so that the brightness will remain where before there was a body. It is what urges human beings to procreate out of fear that life will put an end to them. It is the inspiration of the poet, who translates his feeling into words of love, so that it will not stagnate and die. It is the power of the soul, which makes its way through the darkness of our matter, valiantly imposing itself by its natural superiority.

The will is all this and much more; and in the case that concerns us here, it is the energy we put into the game of illusion, combining more and more forces so that we can move from the darkness of not knowing to the splendour of wisdom. Maya wilfully applies its tricks, because its will is that our world of matter and form should never disappear, as long as its intelligence lasts and as long as our innocence and ignorant docility do not change.

In the human being, the will appears above and below, in the opaqueness of matter and the ethereality of the soul. If the will descends through the human planes and appears at the lowest levels, this is when the well-known expressions appear, such as: "I want", or "I don't want", "I'm going to do this", or "I'm not going to do such and such a thing anymore". Wanting in a demanding way is the reflection that can be seen of the will once it has descended to the limits of the body and its desires.

However, will is not only about wanting; it is also being able to do what one wants. Will that does not end in action is a force that is wasted, a seed that bears no fruit in the earth. It is like a river that never reaches the sea or a fire without light or heat.

We human beings do little and desire a lot. Our "wants" – a crude imitation of the higher will – occupy almost all of our lives, and the rest of the time is frittered away in imagining that, finally, we have achieved what we wanted so much, or in imagining how much we would suffer if we lost what we might have achieved... And so, in dreams and words, the energy of the will vanishes, that same will that set the Earth in motion, but was unable to make human beings act.

Is there no force in human beings? Yes, there is: the great force of inertia, which has to be conquered so that the will can manifest in its capacity for action.

***

Because of inertia we follow the games of Maya, and we even keep on playing when, logically, we ought to stop... But will enables us to leave the children's game and enter into new cycles of work, always led by the hand of Maya, but one step higher up.

Inertia is heaviness, but it gives way before the changeable winds of Maya. In her eternal revolutions, she makes human beings want one thing today and another tomorrow; the important thing for Maya is that the will should continue to be a child in some human beings who never stopped being children. Today we like one thing, tomorrow another...

When are we going to realize? When will we cease to be a plaything of the illusory winds, swept along by the intrinsic weight of our inertia?

It is not about changing; it is about finding the roots that don't change, so as to allow the joyful growth of leaves and fruits; it is about finding the lasting values, so that the circumstances can always change on the same base, on a single ideal.

***

Maya is full of will, a good example of something that never changes in the midst of perpetual change. Could we conceive of anything more varied than the games of illusion? Can we imagine more colours, more forms, more multiplication than those offered by Maya? Nevertheless, in the midst of this apparent whirlwind, she is firm and sure of the goal that inspires her.

Maya always plays; she never stops playing, even if her toys may vary. Sometimes we love Maya, inspired by her unlimited manifestation, and at other times we hate her when we feel her strong claw holding back our will for liberation. But while we are loving her or hating her, she continues to play with the world and its beings, she continues to lead them towards their destiny of continuous life, of constant reproduction, of incessant multiplication.

If we were to discover the secret of Maya, we would be just like her: wanting today what we wanted yesterday and what we will want tomorrow. Doing things today better than yesterday and better tomorrow than today. Playing, yes, but knowing why we are doing so; with Maya or without her, because that is what we have decided by our own will.

SOCIETY

How can we speak about society without referring to the human being, whom we have already mentioned so many times in this work? Because a society is not something abstract, it is based on its essential component: the human being.

It is Maya who creates societies as well, and she does so because, in order to perpetuate her work, she needs to bring human beings together in groups, she needs to entertain them and make them play with one another. The small family group – the restricted nucleus of two, three or ten individuals – is no longer enough. Now the game requires a much larger number.

Maya needs to form societies and make human beings feel the need to come together in social groups. Society is characterized by a need, but it is not like love, when there is a need for souls to complement one another, or friendship, which brings together complementary virtues. Society's need is the need for biological survival.

There are many things that one person on their own cannot achieve for their survival, either because they don't have the time or energy, or because they lack the necessary knowledge. One person alone cannot obtain for themselves a house, food, clothing, transport, tools... One person alone would not be able to defend themselves or make war. One person can do some of these things well, but not all of them; as a result, individuals exchange their skills with those of others, who provide them with the things they lack.

In this social game there is a strong element of dependency: everyone needs others to be able to exist, if only physically; and for Maya's purposes, the physical aspect represents one of the most important forms of existing.

***

Since when have societies existed? Ever since Maya has been playing... Ever since she brought together several human beings to exchange their skills and share their joys and sorrows.

In the most primitive societies – primitive in terms of possibilities, not in terms of antiquity – the relationship between human beings was limited to an exchange of material goods. But, as societies evolved, together with the evolution of the human beings who formed part of them, other needs appeared. The characteristic of society – need – did not change, but the type of need did.

Among the many skills that came to be needed was the skill of working with more subtle elements, such as justice or the exercise of power. And if the different trades had already been entrusted to the most experienced people, it was accepted as logical that the strongest individual should exercise power on behalf of everyone else and the most just person should exercise justice. When these higher needs came into being, the primitive society was transformed into a state, just as in evolution the passionate human being was transformed into the thinking and rational human being.

Despite the fact that the birth of the state resulted in Maya losing one of her veils, she had to continue to play in this new order of things. How would she do it? By indirectly covering the face of justice and by weakening the sense of power. By making human beings forget that, in order to be suited to these subtle exercises, it is also necessary to become a complete human being; it is no longer enough to have a strong and energetic body; now a healthy psyche and mind are also required, a dose of intuitive intelligence and a good measure of will. And there are few enough of such human beings in the world of Maya...

In this way, states never ceased to be mere societies, where everything can be bought and sold, depending on supply and demand.

***

In the game of society there is no such thing as equality. This is a myth invented by human beings to avoid taking part in the game of Maya; with the difference that Maya is interested in what can be useful to all human beings, while those who invented the myth of equality were interested in the benefit of a few: those who decreed that everyone was equal – apart from themselves, of course.

The simplest logic tells us that, in order for a society – or state – to function, there cannot be equality. There cannot be a game if all the pieces are equal, not because there is no longer any need for the game, but because it has not even started.

To play with external inequalities in order to reach the goal of essential equality is one thing. To ignore the essential equalities – because one is ignorant of the essence of the human being, which is Spirit – in order to enforce superficial equalities, is something quite different. The first is the natural game of life, where one goes from the external to the internal, from the many to the one, from the different to the identical. The second is to break the law of life, to flatten the rich range of possibilities that Nature offers and to make similar human beings slaves in ignorance.

***

With Maya's permission, we are going to try to clarify this thorny issue of equality. Human beings are equal at their two extremes: they have a body with a similar constitution, and similar functions and needs; and they have a spirit that shares the same origin and the same destiny. Between these two poles there is a long series of inequalities, because in the race of life some have evolved more than others: it is not that they are better for no reason; they are better because they have walked more, suffered more, learnt more. And those who have evolved less are not "worse"; they are more like helpless and needy children, who should not be taken advantage of, but educated.

On the basis of these inequalities, Maya was able to form societies, because if we had all been equal, there would have been nothing to share and nothing to exchange. What can we gain from seeing our own reflection repeated thousands of times in as many other mirrors, which are human beings who are the same as us? How can we combine, relate to and be united with what is the same as ourselves?

Inequality is not bad, but can be the starting point for something good, if we can learn how to use all the different pieces of the game in a harmonious way, until they form a meaningful unity. What is bad is not knowing how to play, not knowing how to combine the elements, not knowing how to obtain the final piece, and not wanting to do the work, setting out from the false premise that there is nothing to do.

In the game of Maya there is no equality. She strives, by the use of different lights, colours and shades, nuances and a thousand tricks, to remove the last glimmer of the two equalities that affect living beings and their two poles: above and below, spirit and material support.

One has to feel different in order to take part in the game; different, needing others and complementary.

That is why, in the meantime, and in between the two essential equalities, all we need to do is to play as we evolve. But to play in society.

HUMAN GROUPS

From the individual solitude in which human beings find themselves when, in the midst of the game of Maya, they decide to look inwards for an instant, there is a reaction towards union, which gives rise to society, and a reaction towards order, which results in the state. In this way, human beings believe they can escape from their painful and misunderstood solitude.

But they very soon discover that this was not a real solution to the problem. Although society, with its form of union, and the state, with its ordering laws, include very broad and general human groups, there is no room for the particularities and personal shades of each individual. And so the inverse process begins, where people look for smaller and more specific unions, where forms of work, artistic tastes, interests, studies, beliefs, etc., can be shared.

These associations come into being to alleviate solitude and satisfy certain needs of an individual nature which neither society because of its breadth, nor individuals alone because of their lack of resources, can resolve.

***

Let us use this simile of the state as a human body and think of these various groups we have mentioned as if they were specialized tissues within the body. In this way, groups have the fundamental purpose of carrying out and perfecting their specific function; they are like a healthy heart, well constituted lungs or a stomach that has an excellent capacity to digest and assimilate at the same time.

But let us now suppose that the body becomes ill, in other words, in our analogy, that the state, at its peak, begins to display serious failings. It is logical that as soon as the thinking head of the body fails, the lesser organs will also begin to fail. The stomach will cease to digest correctly, the lungs will barely absorb the pure oxygen, the heart will fail to pump the blood sufficiently... And the disorder of the specialized organs will result in an even greater state of illness for the body in general. It is difficult to decide whether it was the organs that made the body ill or the body that caused the degeneration of the organs. But in the game of Maya, the part that has the greatest capacity shoulders the majority of the blame: the intelligence which co-ordinated the body is the cause, then, of the disorder of the whole and of the parts.

How does illness manifest in human groups? In the same way as in the body. They cease to fulfil their specific functions and gradually lose the spirit of union that once gave birth to them; then they become increasingly divided, just as when the body dies and, one by one, the cells demand their right to independence. They are no longer groupings within the state – organs within the body – but little states or little bodies that attempt to exist autonomously, forgetting that their meaning and purpose derived from their spirit of union.

When the body dies, a veritable war breaks out between the cells; lacking the unifying intelligence that had previously directed them, each one now tries to survive without any regard for the others.

When the state dies and there is only a society, which is a simple aggregation of human beings, this aggregation begins to dissolve, as can be clearly seen in the process suffered by human groups. Before, each one had a value and a task, and between them all they produced a harmonious result. Now, each one wants its part, the best part, and none of them look at what is happening to the others. Each one thinks that it is the group and that all the others are unnecessary in the social landscape; each one believes itself to be the best, the highest, the only one capable of becoming the head, and in this way all of them fight to climb to the top of society, because none of them wants to grow; to climb, just to climb.

The process does not stop here. Once the autonomy of each group has been declared, confrontations within the same group begin to appear. Now it is individuals who oppose one another and fight with determination for a position, an honour, certain privileges, renown and impunity to satisfy all their personal desires.

When the different groups separated from one another, people stopped caring about the state; when conflict arises within a group, people forget about the group and focus on their own individual benefits.

If this increasing struggle is replicated among groups of

relatives, friends, brothers and sisters, we can be sure that the state has died and that all its components are fighting each other in the soil of the tomb, selfishly trying to survive until a new order enables them to participate in a new state, a new integral body.

***

The game of Maya can be seen in all of this. Human beings come together in groups as a game, and as a game they confront one another and separate from one another, as the strange breaths of life pulsate, uniting and disuniting, seeking in each new experience a greater perfection.

Human beings come together because they discover that they need mutual assistance, and then separate on the grounds of a desired self-sufficiency. The game lasts for the lifetime of an individual, or for the lifetime of a state...

But just as the dissolution of the body does not imply the disappearance of the spirit of the human being, so the dissolution of the state and the breaking up of its parts does not signify the death of the spirit of order. The same cycles that Maya presents to us under the form of day and night or the revolving seasons, giving Nature her different forms, also affect all living things; and naturally they affect human beings, their unions, their dreams and their achievements.

Today, Maya has put on the show of trade unions, churches, markets, clubs, political parties – in short, all kinds of groups in which human beings seek to satisfy their biological, psychological, intellectual and, occasionally, spiritual needs, and above all to deaden their sense of solitude.

But has solitude disappeared? On the contrary, in the attempt to reduce it, the many paths have been multiplied and solitude has been atomized into thousands of particles which grow by becoming bigger, spreading the pain more widely.

THE FAMILY

Just mentioning this word calls to mind the many definitions that have been put forward about this "cell of society". Although we should rather speak of a "cell of the state", since it is a small nucleus organized on the basis of aims that go beyond mere physical life. However, Maya has woven her nets, so we shall limit ourselves to considering it as a social cell... unless the games get out of hand and the lack of limits on human action lead it to stop being even a cell.

The family has always been thought of as the most suitable means of escaping from solitude: it is a small group, in which there is a reciprocal exchange of benefits and where the highly valued ties of blood prevail.

But is blood the only and the best bond, that we should give it so much value? Does shared blood necessarily lead to shared tastes, opinions, feelings or ideals? We would very much like to answer in the affirmative, but apart from rare exceptions, daily experience shows us quite the opposite.

It is Maya who has inculcated in the human mind the strong sense of union by blood, because otherwise she would not have found the means to ensure that humans would stay together, have children and bring them up for an appropriate period of time. It is Maya who has made all children seem beautiful, intelligent and exceptional in every respect. It is Maya who makes us try to defend everything relating to the family, giving it priority over whatever else may be happening in the rest of the world.

And Maya knows why she plays with the family: because if these little social centres could achieve their full development, human beings would be much better prepared to live together in general and to establish good states.

***

For the moment, however, while we play at making families, we are continuing to learn how to live and we tend to ignore many paradoxes and illnesses that undermine our fundamental social cell.

So, in order to play better, let us look at the mistakes we make and how we can improve our behaviour, even in the world of Maya.

***

Carried away by the illusion that everything can be bought and sold, that everything has a price, we have also applied this concept to the family. Consequently, the family has become one of the many forms of ownership: parents own their children; the husband owns his wife and vice versa; the children "have" their parents, and so on.

It is no longer a case of a natural feeling of belonging, but of things becoming complicated when the "owner" attempts to make the one who is "owned" do everything that is demanded of them. If the husband asks something of his wife, there will always be some who remind him that she also has the right to ask for something. If the parents ask their children to do something, or to study some subject, the children reply that it is they, the parents, who should give in to their wishes, since the children "did not ask to be born"; they were "forced to come into the world".

In this way, everyone asks, everyone demands, everyone tries to give orders to others, but no one actually does anything. There is a lack of true comradeship, which is the original sense of family. People only look for benefits; no one wants to give; and if the mother gives her whole heart to her child, it is because Maya has covered her eyes with the most delicate veils so that life can continue. Let us wait for a while and we will see how the veils become torn little by little, and what had been an unbreakable bond begins to show cracks on the path of mutual demands that arise over time.

***

While we play at making families, it is more and more common for parents to have nothing in common – apart from ties of blood – with their children. There is nothing to prevent educated, honest and spiritual parents having unruly and uncultured children on whom education has little effect and who laugh at the tastes of their parents. On the other hand, hard-nosed parents dedicated to the pursuit of wealth may produce children who are sensitive to things of the soul, to beauty and justice.

The tradition of the whole family coming together at mealtimes has become no more than a slow torture, where no one knows what to talk about in order to avoid hurting each other's feelings, at least when there is some vestige of politeness. Otherwise, mealtimes are the times for arguments, anxieties, confrontations, harsh words... and bad digestion.

***

We said that while we are playing at making families we are gradually learning to live; that we have not yet created ordered families – in the style of the state – but social families, where the needs for subsistence prevail.

It is here that the greatest danger lies: the loss of the hierarchical order in the family. Parents are not parents and children are not children. The former lack the moral strength to educate, while the latter do not have good examples to learn from.

The 'water of learning' no longer flows from above to below, no longer goes from parents to children. To educate implies a good deal of self-sacrifice on the part of the parents, because they have to improve their own personalities so that they will always give a good image to their children; and how many parents are prepared to make such a sacrifice? To learn implies a measure of admiration for their parents on the part of the children, but what can they admire if they see them constantly arguing, allowing themselves to be dominated by their passions, trying to avoid their responsibilities?

There is no great distance from here to arrive at new paradoxes: the adults play at being young, trying to look like their children, speaking in inappropriate ways and worrying about things that should only concern adolescents. For their part, young people play at being old, destroying their clothes until they appear poor and torn, colouring their hair and taking drugs to escape from the "terrible responsibility that life represents". Of course, in this way neither adults nor adolescents fulfil their roles in the family, or even in the society in which they live.

This total lack of organization, this family anarchy, means that there is only one thing to share in the family unit: the lack of respect.

***

Faced with this heartbreaking spectacle, and knowing Maya, who never makes mistakes in her actions, we ask ourselves: has the family been lost, or is this just a case of people unsuccessfully trying to simulate family life? We incline towards the second possibility.

We believe that not all families are formed with sufficient care and dedication. When as children we used to play at "mamas and papas", we would prepare a good place, we would choose dolls, utensils and all the necessary items to "set up a home". But when we grow up, we don't do the same. We have lost the ability to play and we don't understand why we should take part in the game.

In many cases, families arise by "chance", because "you have to get married", and the children come into being by the same law of chance which caused a man and a woman to meet each other, rather as if someone might trip on a stone on a corner. But that should not be sufficient reason to form a family.

We know that there are many difficulties involved in setting up the ideal family unit, ranging from the economic to the spiritual, from not having enough money to keep up payments on a mortgage to the fear of living together completely; but all these difficulties can be overcome if one has the firm and unshakeable will of wanting to set up a family.

Even the humblest craftsman imagines his work before he begins. How, then, can we avoid planning something as important as the work of art of the family?

***

Although Maya wants to perpetuate and multiply bodies, and protects the family with this intention, she does not prevent souls from coming together as well as bodies. She does not claim that the bond of blood should exclude that other, philosophical bond, in which the family resonates with the same ideas, respects the personalities of each of its members and works together harmoniously in a joint task of the greatest importance: the little state which makes the great state, the modest cell that composes the body of humanity.

In this special kind of family, the parents educate because they have first worked on themselves. The children learn from their parents with the same admiration with which they can look up at the stars in the sky. The parents know by experience the appropriate way to explain things, and the children have the patience that their youth demands to know everything at the right time. The brothers and sisters love each other because they share something more than the same room. The state of all of them living together is expressed in giving and receiving with equal joy and with an identical knowledge of what it means to be alive, to grow, to be able to achieve everything that has been dreamt of.

It is precisely in this way that Maya forms families with all the humans who play in her nets.

EDUCATION

We return to that old formula that states that “to educate” is “to educe”, to draw out from within the human being the great wealth of experience accumulated over time; and once educed, it needs to be put it into practice so that we can live better.

We all want to live, but it is also necessary to know how to live. A well-educated person lives in his completeness, both in his lower polarity of matter and in the higher polarity of spirit. An uneducated person, or someone with nothing to educe, is only half alive and usually lives wherever the weight obliges him to fall: in the physical world.

Maya has a very particular concept of life: she knows that life is in all things and that there are subtle planes where bodies are not needed. But she has been given the task of looking after bodies, looking after the material world, and that is what she does conscientiously. As a result, she has made human beings accustomed to only looking after the life of dense matter, and therefore to educating that matter.

***

Let us come out of the game of Maya for a moment and look at how children are educated. No effort is spared in teaching them how to eat, to dress, to wash, to use the things they need;

their carers are concerned about their growth, their health, their beauty, the pleasure they can obtain... but always on the outside, always aimed at the satisfaction of the body. Of the rest of the person nothing is known, and if there is an intuition of something else, they try to ignore it as if it did not exist.

What is more, as an intrinsic part of this game, there are parents who know they could educate something more than the surface of their children, but do not do so out of fear. They fear that their children might become "different", that if they were to live for their inner world they would suffer from the indifference or misunderstanding of others. And they deprive their children of a priceless treasure which, certainly, could make them different, but also better.

***

If to educate is to educe, and to educe means to allow that which lies deep within to emerge, it is evident that, to be able to educate, we must accept that there is something more at work within human beings than their vital organs. That "something" is like the core that defines us; it is our oldest self, that self which holds the memory of many worlds and paths, that self which – even if we appear not to remember – has gathered fruits along all the ways of the earth. And that inner "something" knows because it is old, because it has lived so much and because of all the things it has accumulated in the time it has lived. And that is what manifests when it is educated.

***

There are formulas that enable us to educe. We have to know some secrets, like someone who knows how to crack a nut in order to extract the kernel, or someone who knows how to peel a potato in order to eat the inside, or how to break the shell of an egg in order to make use of its yolk. Although we have learned to peel potatoes, break eggs and crack nuts, we lack formulas for gathering the inner fruit of the human being. We work with human beings as if we were only concerned with polishing the outside of nuts, potatoes or eggs, completely unaware of what is contained beneath the covering. But the heart knows more than the skin, and the soul knows more than the body.

Why do we not have formulas to educate? Because, blinded by the game of Maya, we have destroyed the better part of the human being. Because no one looks after their own psyche, or their mind, or their spirit, so it is difficult to gather experiences in that sense, experiences that would become transmissible to others.

A person who works with wood thinks every day about the successes he has obtained and takes care not to make mistakes; he knows the grains of the matter with which he works and if he had an apprentice beside him, he could teach him everything he has gathered in his continuous experience. But if human beings do not work on their inner wood, what can they observe? What can they gather? What can they transmit?

And when human beings do not work on their inner wood, if they are not familiar with that area of their being, even if the highest Master were to come and explain the mysteries of education to them, they would not be able to apply his teachings. They would not understand anything. They would not believe anything they were hearing.

If there are no human beings with inner life, there can be no education that will awaken the inner life in others.

Today parents can give physical life, but it is rare that they can give birth to the inner being. Today teachers can train their students, they can teach them to carry out certain tasks efficiently, but they cannot educate.

***

Undoubtedly, Maya prefers uneducated human beings; she prefers those simple little animals that only know about subsisting and working in order to offer worship to the god that Maya serves: matter. Maya plays with tamed human beings as in a circus: she needs people who can use their bodies perfectly, but don't want to know why they do so; their eyes are blindfolded, as a symbol that the less they see, the less they risk their physical structures, led on by an ancestral automatism, which moves things without knowing what movement is.

Will there ever be a Prometheus who, out of pity for human misery, brings light into this world? Will Maya herself at any time pick up a torch in her hands and allow human beings to see, finally, the meaning and purpose of her rhythmic dance?

If this could happen, if at some point a part of the veil were to be lifted, there would be some educated person who would start a new chain, whose links would not be free from the game, but they would learn to look at the inner workings of their toys.

SCIENCE

This is an ordered and systematic form of knowledge, which is like a spear-point that can tear open the veils with which Maya covers her game. Science is one of the ways in which, through Maya, we can understand truth.

But it does not suit the designs of Maya for a true science to exist, as this would be equivalent to losing her hidden secrets. That is why she entertains herself by entangling the threads of knowledge and providing a game for human beings that acts as a substitute for science.

***

Much of science works with numbers, and numbers are abstractions that we never fully understand. Between one number and another lies a hidden infinity that nothing can fill, and we even have a vague intuition that the so-called numerical digits are not simply the result of the accumulation or addition of units. To add up two things of the same nature is simple, but if we try to add up abstract units, what is the result? And how could we add up things of a different nature?

One of the characteristics of science is the requirement that its knowledge should always be exact. In science there are no relatives, no intermediate states. But if science applies to our world, and this world is full of relatives, how can we make it exact just by measuring it with numbers? There is something in this whole process that gives us the impression of someone trying to fit a big foot into a small shoe.

It would be good to apply the principle of exactness to the great laws of Nature. But it is difficult for our current science to accept these laws; and even these laws govern living beings. So, we can observe that the laws vary from time to time in response to the rhythms and necessities of life, such as when the Earth alters its speed of rotation around the Sun in order to avoid a collision with a comet. Where was the exactness in this case? In the fact that it altered its usual speed or in the fact that it avoided the collision?

Anyone who speaks of exactness should also remember another of the games of Maya that she likes to play: infallibility. Science never mistakes, they say. Once certain hypotheses have been put forward and these arguments have been proven – more or less successfully – nothing can be said against them, because they represent the only truth.

But do these worshippers of the infallible not remember that each generation believed the same about the things that it had been able to discover?

Is it not a sign of ignorant conceit to attribute complete certainty to things that are almost completely unknown?

***

For the science of Maya, what is not known does not exist. There may be cases in their thousands, inexplicable situations that cry out for an explanation, but if this science has not yet concerned itself with the phenomenon, then the phenomenon does not exist.

One day, someone will “discover” an “explanation” among the infinite veils of Maya, and then, that which did not exist or had no value at all will suddenly come to life. It is like saying that light did not exist until someone could establish certain laws about how it operates; or like completely denying the speed of sound until it has been measured.

The science of Maya has forgotten how to recognize what is not known, to take it as a starting point for research, and so enable us to know more things than those which are understood today.

This systematic denial of what is unknown often leads to falsified research, where the result is known even before the research begins: it has to be proven that what was said not to exist does not really exist. To that end, any distortion, fraud or self-deception is admitted, so that no one has to say: “I don’t know”. More than research, we can refer to such cases as social conditioning, satisfaction of vanity, but never as healthy “philosophy”, or love of wisdom.

***

Another mystery that surrounds the distorted science of our illusory world is to believe that it is incompatible with everything that has to do with art and beauty, poetry and imagination. Science, in order to qualify as such, must be cold and harsh, devoid of harmony; its concepts must be crudely expressed and it criticizes the ancient civilizations precisely for their capacity to combine what is beautiful with what is useful.

In this way, scientists are prevented from understanding anything about the arts and, if they are moved by beauty, they must seriously reconsider their attitude: perhaps it means that they were not born to research and discover the truth. At the other extreme, we have artists who despise order and method, and believe that a number or a formula will ruin their work forever. Oh, Maya, how you play with us when you don't want us to know about your reality!

Let us try to distinguish between the great science and the lesser science with which Maya keeps us constantly entertained.

The great science is that which made Socrates say: "I only know that I know nothing". It is only from that position that we can start to make progress, because this affirmation-negation contains a principle of truth. With this principle of truth we can pull on the thread that leads to the centre. From here it is possible to make our way towards the All, towards Unity, towards a vision of the universe as a whole, which is known as a cosmovision or cosmic worldview.

The lesser science is that which wants to know ever smaller and more limited things. It is based on the illusion of dividing things in order to know them better. But in this case it is not a graduated division – from the whole to the part – but a confrontation between the particles of knowledge which, as they become increasingly separated, oppose one another.

This division, which is managed – as usual – by Maya, does not prevent things from being joined together again, and while we human beings distract ourselves by researching the microparticles of the universe, Maya continues to maintain her necessary realm.

***

As long as there is no cosmovision, there will be no great science, no wisdom. And even when Maya keeps it hidden, she shows with her actions that knowledge is power. And knowing things well gives the power to act well.

RELIGION

More than a game, religion is a support that Maya places in the world that enables human beings to reach God.

Although Maya works tirelessly to ensure that human beings recognize the god for whom she works – matter, life, reproduction of forms, growth – through this god we can come to conceive that other, absolute God, because the wonders of matter and the laws that govern it point to another intelligent marvel that moves the whole.

It is not as some believe, when blinded by the game, that merely by looking at matter we become more materialistic; for those whose eyes are accustomed to the dazzling brightness of Maya, the perfection of matter is proof of the existence of a higher 'That' which was able to programme that matter.

Specific religions, specific names, particular representations, explanatory symbols, rituals laid down by tradition: this is the complex ceremony that human beings establish on earth so that they can be heard by God in heaven. Everyone must be spoken to in their own language, and human beings feel that symbols are the language that is best suited to their ceremony of coming closer to the Deity.

However, as there are many human beings and Maya has accustomed them to division, so, on the religious plane, the many human beings have tried to divide their opinions about which symbols are most appropriate for representing the framework of the Divinity. Some choose certain symbols, others choose others, and the religious language is complicated by an infinite number of symbolic elements. Ceremonies become more and more separated from one another, even if they all claim to be addressing God.

But when the ceremony becomes internal, when the name, the attribute, the image and the virtue are felt to be living in our own heart, when we perform a ceremony from that human point where the human touches the divine, then the different religions fade away and the One God becomes light for the higher intuition.

***

But it does not yet suit Maya that human beings should succeed in discovering the secret of unity. For now, it is necessary to play with the many forms, and for human beings to live clinging to their particular belief. Unity is a strong wine for small men.

Maya prefers multiplicity and that each human being should vigorously defend their particle of multiplicity. The game sometimes becomes so disturbing that, in the name of the same Name, people fight and kill one another, because no one stops to think that 'That' which contains all names is not concerned about what we call it, but rather about the way in which, in its name, we act.

One day, all the religious particles will come together, when each of them has become pure, good and strong; and then, between all of them, it will be possible to constitute the great body of the universal religion.

Today, as we are far from that final goal, human beings play with the small bodies of the religions; they play at fighting, defending, winning and losing, without really understanding the meaning and purpose of such a struggle.

While some people defend one form of God, others incline towards another, although the most important thing is that, behind the variety of forms, people should feel and live the need for religion, for "re-union" with the spiritual origin of the human being. Everyone, in one way or another, needs that umbilical cord which, unlike the one which emerges from the body, is never cut.

And let no one say lightly that "religion is the opium of the people"; and that, as it is an umbilical cord, it is better to cut it quickly in order to reach maturity. Just as being born is about more than simply cutting the baby's physical dependency on its mother; and just as children need their parents throughout their lives if they have been able to generate new and positive links with them; so, to be born into conscious life is much more than to "play at being grown-ups" and pretend that we don't need the support of God.

From the spiritual point of view, we are nothing but delicate embryos in the process of formation. This world of Maya, where truth becomes blurred and confused, is the womb in which we are forged, and our umbilical cord is religion, which should lead us gradually to conscious individualization, and the recognition – through evolution – of the Father-Mother whom we sometimes call God.

ART

In the world of the archetypes there is an ideal beauty that is difficult to translate into words, since it escapes the poor capacity of definition of human beings. Nevertheless, human beings do tend to intuit something of that ideal beauty and try to reproduce it in matter. That material expression of an ideal beauty is what we call art.

Thus, for art to exist, we need two factors: a higher beauty and the matter in which it can be given form.

The laws of art do not come from matter, however, but from the ideal world where beauty resides; matter can only show us the limits to artistic inspiration.

That is why not all so-called artists are truly artists; we cannot refer in the same way to those who use matter as a support, but are inspired by higher archetypes, and those others who use matter as a support and also get their inspiration from it. To be able to discover the laws that belong to the archetypal world, artists must have awakened as human beings: they must have developed their noblest sentiments to a high degree, as well as a good deal of intelligence, intuition and will to create.

For her part, Maya makes sure that there are not many of these true artists, because the world of beauty and the discovery of its essential harmony are among the extraordinary keys that allow human beings to enter into her mystery. It suits Maya to have the artists of matter, those who play with her world of varied forms, those who amuse themselves with lights and colours, imagining that they can change them at their pleasure.

***

Living in the world of Maya, there is no other option but to participate in her game. Here, art too is a game, by means of which "artists" attempt to copy the forms of Nature. But this is copying, not creation. While Nature has the gift of creation, those who play at art can only imitate what they see, what they hear, what they touch. But as they are imitating without knowing the truth of what they are imitating, they frequently distort what they perceive.

Nevertheless, the art of copying has its difficulties, as it is not as simple as it seems to reproduce the forms of Nature. When it proves very difficult to copy, fantasy comes to the aid of the minor artist and "deforms the forms" in whatever way feels best to him. Instead of making an effort to grasp them in their perfection, he reduces them to the level of an imitation. Such artists do not imitate what they see, but present what they want to see. And what people usually see tends to be distorted by the veils with which Maya covers our ignorance.

But these players at art have found a good means of expression for these deformations which they apply to the world around them: they say that they are not reproducing what is outside, but the image that the outer world projects within themselves. Thus, they paint, engrave, draw, write, compose music, according to the reflections they see in themselves.

Ah, mystery of mirrors! What strange images can be produced by the inner windows of human beings! How much cleaning will be necessary so that at least the inner image may show something of clarity and sharpness! How much vanity there is in those who prefer to copy what is in themselves to copying what old and wise Nature has prepared for us over so many millennia!

***

And since we have opened this door to the world of Maya, let us use this opportunity to recall something about the art of the word. The Tower of Babel was also the work of Maya: a single language, a single speech... that is not good for encouraging the childish curiosity of the human being, who still needs many experiences in this world.

Ever since then, Maya has been mixing up many verbal expressions, and a single word means many things; and a single thing can be said with many words.

We know nothing about how to call each thing by its true name, but Maya knows how to call us by our own.

We know nothing of the higher art in which sound is a vehicle of understanding, in which the word is an intelligent sound. On the contrary, our sounds are still very similar to shouting, and our written word can be like a wounding spear hidden in the paper.

Have we ever given ourselves time to listen to the delicate symphony that Maya plays with the whole of Nature?

***

Maya is the most excellent artist that can be conceived. There is no form of art that is forbidden to her; she is the lady and mistress of Nature and knows how to play with all her forms. She shines and lets her light go out, she sings and falls silent, bursts into flower and hides, cries and laughs, rises with the sun, as well as with the moon, paints her world in an infinity of shades of colour.

Maya acts and, like an artist of genius, keeps human beings enraptured by her extraordinary performance. Maya is beautiful, and in her beauty she keeps human beings in the thrall of her harmonious features. Maya is strong, and shows that nothing in the world can stand against her, and as a result she wins the admiration that human beings lavish on the strong.

Maya protects art, because – let us remember – this is one of her doors.

POLITICS

This is a science and also an art: a science, because it requires stable and clearly defined knowledge about human leadership; an art, because inspiration is needed to know how to apply the rules of science.

What is politics about? The leadership of nations, but a leadership which is closely linked to education; it is about teaching human beings about an upward path that will remove the pain of ignorance and lift them up towards the peaks of human destiny.

If this leadership is to be legitimate, the person who leads or guides others must be one who knows how to do so and is able to do so because they have passed the prior test of learning to lead themselves. Someone who cannot or does not know how to do this is led. There is no privilege or dishonour in being one who leads or one who is led; it is simply a case of each one occupying their natural place.

If – taking a simile from many of the great teachers who have existed in the world – we compare nations to flocks of sheep, who leads whom? Does the shepherd lead the sheep or do the sheep lead the shepherd?

***

If we look at it in this way, it all seems very simple, but in the webs of Maya everything becomes complicated. And politics has been complicated to inconceivable limits.

In the first place, it is almost impossible to speak of nations, and far less to compare them in a healthy way to flocks of sheep. There are no longer any shepherds; only sheep are left. And then, which of the sheep will be the one to lead, if they are all more or less the same and all of them harbour the same ambitions to stand out?

Secondly, there is no wisdom in leadership; there are only opinions, and opinions are as changeable as the winds, because they are not based on truth, but on fashions, whims, convenience, needs.

Finally, there is no goal to lead people towards. What is the purpose of such leadership? Where shall we lead them? That is why there is no leadership, that is why states fail, that is why there are only conglomerations of human beings and attempts at societies.

So, let us not refer to politics – to the science and art – but to the fancy dress party which is normally held in its name.

Each sheep in the flock plays at dressing up as the shepherd, with more or less success, and all the sheep await their turn to show off in front of the others, wearing clothes and attributes that don't belong to them. But what does it matter, if there is no shepherd?

The rules of this game consist mainly of lies and falsehood; in one way or another, the truth must be disguised, and we are not referring here to any absolute truth, but to the simple truth that arises from a harmony between what we say and what we do. Those who disguise themselves in this game deceive people consciously, not in the way that Maya does, seducing her creatures in order to keep them on the earth and help them to live, but with a dangerous manipulation that puts others' lives at risk.

People play at growing, but all they do is get fatter. They don't grow upwards, there is no vertical expansion in which human beings can express themselves on all the planes of their being; they walk horizontally, imagining decorative hills to replace the painful effort of climbing.

There is no vocation for service; there is a thirst for business. The person who dresses up as a shepherd does not do so to help others in whatever way he can, but tries to obtain every possible benefit that this fraudulent situation offers him.

And to complete the danger, this game of fancy dress and lies is lacking in all ideology; there seems to be no other purpose apart from the profit of those who claim to be the leaders. It is true that Maya also disguises herself and deceives, but her ideal is profound; she wants to perpetuate the forms of life, not for herself, but for the benefit of life itself, for all living beings, to make Nature everlasting.

At no point in this political game is there any factor that addresses the invisible human being, the one who is not made of flesh and blood; there is nothing for his soul, there is nothing for his better education, there is nothing for the future, because the dressed up sheep have no time to think about what will happen tomorrow. They have dressed up today, and they want to reap their rewards today.

Maya is a great politician of life. She knows how to lead her human beings, she knows how she does it, why she is doing it and where she is leading them. Maya educates them while she plays and provides them with experiences while she entertains them.

But Maya is shocked at this other game of human beings...

Or is it the case that, when the final hour of a civilization strikes, Maya entangles and obstructs the threads of political leadership so that the edifice will fall, while we human beings carry on with the sense that we are managing and saving the process?

WAR

On many occasions, throughout these pages dedicated to Maya, we have spoken about the duality of spirit and matter, and one might think that this is the only form of opposition in manifestation. But Maya, who works in the world of matter, also presents a duality which, though illusory, is fundamental in the eyes of human beings: that of life and death. We call life the appearance in matter, and death the disappearance on that same plane.

Maya works on the basis of this dual game. Death is linked to war, and life to love. But, as life and death are two sides of the same coin – the coin of the One Life – war and love are also facets of one and the same thing.

No two things are apparently more different than war and love, and yet they are of the same essence, based on the same game of appearing and disappearing.

Maya builds and destroys; the two poles of this question are in her hands: she gives life and takes life away following an identical rule of the game. It reminds us of the story of Penelope and her eternal weaving and unravelling, because she needed to delay the men who were importuning her. Maya weaves and unravels the threads of life, because she needs to entertain the human beings who are undergoing their experiences in this world of matter.

She builds with the illusion of love. She destroys with the other illusion of war.

All war is destruction and death, but when referring to war we should not only think of the war which is waged in bloody battles by human beings. There is warfare at all levels of life.

The seed that breaks open to give birth to the tree is at war. The male and female cells that battle one another to give rise to a third life are at war. The big fish that eats the little one; the strong animal that pursues the weaker but faster animal – all of them are at war. The wind that pulls the leaves off the trees, the rain that makes the earth wet, also fight with one another... Even the galaxies have their own special forms of confrontation, which result in the light-emitting deaths of hundreds of stars and planets.

Is there any part of Nature, from the smallest to the largest beings, where we do not see examples of this fate?

***

Duality is not content with being dual; as well as being dual, it needs to create an opposition between its two principles so that each of them can become stronger and surer of itself. Thus, the reason for opposition, for the perpetual war of Nature, is to be found in duality.

The history of humanity itself is a reflection of these permanent oppositions, and there is no way of narrating history that is not based on some kind of opposition. There have always been builders of pyramids and destroyers of pyramids... and these two have always confronted one another, in an attempt to ensure that one of them should prevail for longer.

There have always been struggles between those who follow the impulse of matter and those who seek the force of the spirit. In one way or another, this distinction has been expressed in all the actions of human beings and in the whole of history that they have written, are writing now and will write in the future.

***

There is also war within the human being; in our own micro-universe there is a long-standing opposition between our heaven and our earth, between our higher self and our small everyday self. It seems impossible to speak of two "selves" within the human being or, if there are two selves, we think they would have to be of the same nature. But this is not the case. The duality that pervades the whole world has also been imprinted on the human sphere. One thing is the personal and egotistical self, which seeks only the satisfaction of its own desires and wants; and something very different is the self that aspires to great ideals and fights for great achievements that will benefit the whole of humanity rather than just one individual. And these two "selves" oppose one another, each trying to become stronger in the battle.

If we extend this individual confrontation to wider spheres, we will be able to understand how, if there is war in a single human being, war may also exist between several human beings. It will help us understand why brothers fight against brothers, why there are civil wars between citizens of a single nation; why there are bloodthirsty wars between one nation and another, although they apparently belong to the same humanity.

The fact is that the builders of pyramids and the destroyers of pyramids oppose one another wherever they meet, whether it is within an individual, within a family, within a nation or within the whole of humanity.

***

Beyond the veil of Maya, we can see a game of successive and necessary destructions that lead to major renewals: it is like the old skin that falls off to give place to the new one.

However, at the current crossroads of history, this deeper sense of war has been lost, and the game which is played out today is a rapid destruction, without the consequent renewal. We already know that it is much easier to destroy than to create...

In other cases, what is proposed as a renewal turns out to be much worse than the thing it replaced. War, like every magical act within Nature, must have a useful purpose: if something is broken, it must be replaced, and if it is replaced, what is achieved must be not only new, but better than what went before. Why fight if the new skin will be the same as the previous one? Why fight if sometimes the new skin is worse than the old one, or there is even no new skin to replace it with?

Senseless destruction brings us into the presence of a dangerous instinct: that of death for death's sake. It is the tiredness of old forms that have not been renewed for a long time and unconsciously seek their own destruction so that they can attain a well-deserved rest. Then, after the end of a cycle, the day of a new civilization will dawn.

***

Today, war does not exist. Today, there are no real oppositions. Today everyone fights for the same thing: for a soulless power, for a wealth which is no longer used to adorn the gods, for domination by force without wisdom.

That is why there is no war today: because there is no honour. And for the same reason there is no love.

Nevertheless, in the depths of all beings, the old love for war, the inevitable love between Mars and Venus, continues to breathe. There is still a need for combat, for renewal, for redemption.

But, as there are no great ideals to fight for, people fight for petty interests. And, in the same way, they love trivial things.

***

In whose favour does Maya intervene in this constant combat of Nature? As we said at the beginning, she works with both of them, with war and love, with life and death, because both aspects are contained within her dual world of illusion. She protects any form of duality that contributes to keeping human beings trapped in this life of experiences.

Maya is in favour of matter, essentially because she is matter in action; matter is her reason for being. At the same time, she is not against spirit, because she does not perceive it, even if it is her innermost root; Maya simply hides spirit.

Maya is like a mirror, halfway along the road. Through the mirror we cannot see the spirit. In the mirror we only see the interplay of shapes, lights and colours: these are the weapons with which Maya takes part in the war of the game of existence.

But despite everything, the inverted images of this mirror allow us to have an intuition of what is hidden behind it. It is a question of fighting valiantly to get past the barrier.

LOVE

As we have just seen, love seems to be the polar opposite of war. But in love is also hidden another duality, which gives rise to a middle way. Love lies between pleasure and pain. Between what makes us excessively happy and what wounds us deeply, there is space for the serene simplicity of love.

Pleasure and pain are merely emotions; they are changeable and not in any way lasting. There is nothing more unstable than a pleasure, which does not even completely manage to be a pleasure, because while we are enjoying it, we are already suffering from the fear of losing it. That is why pleasure and pain always go hand in hand.

Amidst the changeability of these two extreme emotions, we find love, as an expression of a higher sentiment.

Today, love is the most overused word and the least felt sentiment. Everyone speaks about love and the great feeling they are experiencing, but the more they speak, the more they demonstrate the lack of love they have, because we all speak about what we lack rather than about what we have.

The difficulty in truly feeling love lies in the fact that, in order to do so, we need to have a great deal of harmony; we must first have recognized in ourselves the endless game of Maya, which leads us from one extreme to another, from pleasures to pains, never allowing us to settle into the stability of the completeness of love.

In love there is room for everything: a degree of pleasure which makes it dream; a degree of pain which makes it experience.

***

Love is a profound need for union with what we lack. Although love is the ultimate feeling, it is at the same time a manifestation of what we human beings lack. We do not love what we have; what we have is simply with us or within us; it is part of ourselves. We love what we lack, what we need, what we want to attract towards ourselves with the strong arms of desire.

We love what completes us, what gives us what we don't have. That is why a man loves a woman, and a woman loves a man. That is why the ignorant person loves wisdom and becomes a "philosopher", and it is also why the wise person loves the innocence of ignorance. It is why the parent loves the child, and the child the parent. It is why Maya loves her human beings, and human beings love the illusion which Maya produces in them.

***

Love with pain is the best form of experience. Although we human beings reject pain as something bad, it is like a bitter medicine which, nevertheless, brings us the health of knowledge. If it were not for pain, we would never pay attention to the things around us or to ourselves.

Love has something of pain. We suffer because of what we

lack; we suffer when we have what we formerly lacked, because now we might have to lose it; and we suffer when we lose what we had because we no longer have it. But wanting, possessing and losing is the way in which we humans learn something from the illusory game of Maya and from the amazing toys she places in our hands.

Love with pleasure is the most wonderful mask with which Maya can present herself. Who wants to reject pleasure? This is the mask with which life protects life, it is the formula of procreation.

Without the mask of pleasure, no one would feel sufficient love in advance to bring a new being into the world; pleasure is the veil that induces us to multiply.

Then comes the love-protection for the little newborn beings – another veil to save the young lives; it is the "love of the parents", who always see the little children they have to raise as beautiful and intelligent.

Finally, it is possible that true love may awaken when the parents need to see themselves perpetuated in the child, and love the child who is a continuation of themselves; and when the children need the support and experience of the parents and love what they teach them. Here, the veil of pleasure has already been drawn back. What remains is a pure, natural, human sentiment.

***

We said that love seeks what it needs or lacks in order to achieve completeness. That is why love is a powerful force that attracts things, joins opposites, combines them, unites them and complements them, in such a way that, where there were two objects, now there is only one. It is like a magnet that seeks and captures its counterpart.

Looking at the life of Maya, we see how the body "loves" the food that it needs to survive. Looking beyond the game of Maya, we see how the soul loves the God it lost in its descent.

***

Love is expressed in a higher way when it is realized in action, when it passes from desire for what is necessary, to becoming one with what is necessary within oneself. Every act of love is an act that leads us naturally towards a greater perfection, towards a more complete development.

And love is expressed in a higher way when it sets its sights on the highest objects, when it learns to look upwards, piercing the veils of Maya with acute vision, when it dreams of and desires to achieve noble ideals.

Then it enters into action, it flies on the wings of will, it attains the ideal that it desired so ardently, becomes one with it and makes it part of its own soul, "its own flesh and blood". That person knows love. That person is an idealist, who not only loves, but also works intensely for what he or she loves. Like Maya, like the illusion which so adores its world and continually works to weave the subtle webs of existence.

DESTINY

Since we are immersed in the attractions of Maya's games, we tend to view destiny as a form of accident, a kind of roulette or lottery, where human beings are allotted more or less happiness by the vagaries of chance.

But if we attempt to draw back a little the veils of Maya, as we have been doing in these pages, so as to understand the meaning and purpose of her game, we will see that there is no such thing as chance, but on the contrary, an evident causality, an order, a law that determines everything that happens.

Chance does not exist, although Maya gives the impression of the contrary; there is only ignorance of the causes of things. The fact that we, as human beings, are unable to understand the purpose of the game of Maya, to understand why she does what she does and moves in the direction she is going in, does not necessarily mean that Maya is ruled by chance.

To deny destiny and to make the whole world subject to chance is the worst symptom of ignorance, of a lack of conscious observation of Nature; and to this we could even add a conscious and unconscious laziness so that we don't have to bother to discover any of the mysteries that trouble us. Are there mysteries? Well, they continue to exist; but by denying them, the lazy person has solved the problem.

***

Destiny is the route marked out by the law of evolution. It is an ascending route of effort, where each step implies the overcoming of a previous stage. But if it were presented so crudely and bleakly, no one would want to travel that road, no one would find sufficient strength within themselves to do it.

This is where Maya intervenes and adorns the path with all kinds of tricks, with a thousand and one artifacts to play with and even to make us believe that we have the power to create on that path. Similarly, no one notices that the path is bordered on both its sides by thick elastic walls which ensure that anyone who, in their unconsciousness, comes dangerously close to the edges, is sent back to the centre of the route. Every attempt to deviate from the line marked out bounces off the elastic walls, so that they understand that there is only one route possible.

We may walk faster or slower; we may pause to rest at some bend in the road; we may try to get closer to the walls on either side of it; we may walk on foot or on our knees, crying or laughing; but we cannot avoid the destiny of human beings... although Maya tries to make the journey as pleasant as possible.

Where does this destiny finally lead? How does this game end? Although we may have a vague intuition about it, we really know nothing for certain. And if we did know, with the weak will that we have, it is very likely that we would want to abandon the race, thus losing the opportunity of being human, of fulfilling our destiny.

***

I think we would all find it easier to accept the concept of destiny if it did not present us with a number of serious difficulties.

In the first place, we don't know where that path began; we don't know where we have come from. Nor do we know where the path is leading; we don't know where we are going. We have a sense of a long memory of the past, which takes the form of vague reminiscences that suddenly explode in our soul; and we also have a presentiment of an infinite future full of opportunities. But here we are in the middle of the journey, without any clear picture, unable to define anything with our mind about what is happening to us, not even the present moment where we are now; in other words, we don't know who we are, or why we are here.

This is a sign that we are sleepwalking, and it is a blessing that the path is enclosed by walls, so that we won't leave it altogether. Our life is a nightmare of unconsciousness, added to which are the veils and artificial lights of Maya, who also attempts by all means to keep us on the path, at least on that part of it for which she is responsible.

If we were able to wake up, we would walk with more confidence, and even if we could still not make out the absolute end of the path, the game would now be different. It would be about reaching the next stage of the route, as if it were the end; once we arrive at that point, we will set ourselves the goal of reaching another section of the path, and so on successively until we complete the whole, guided by hiatuses which, though not definitive, are at least useful.

***

If we know we are asleep, if we know that Maya is playing with us as we travel along the path of destiny, how can we know if we are travelling in the right way, if we are not deviating too many times, if we are doing what we ought to do?

There is an infallible sign that informs us: pain.

There are only two types of beings who do not feel pain: those who are unconscious and those who have freed themselves from error. Assuming that we have already left behind the stage of total unconsciousness, and knowing that the human being is still subject to error, it is impossible to avoid pain.

But, rather than disparaging it, we should accept it as a guiding light on the path, as a light that shows us our mistakes, as an alarm signal that leads us to review our actions and correct our mistakes.

If we don't experience pain, it implies that we are fulfilling our destiny well. If there is a lot of pain, we still need to open our eyes to see clearly where our steps are leading.

***

We shouldn't think that destiny is a cruel master who gives few opportunities – let alone just one – to poor blind humans who are travelling along its ways. On the contrary, there are many – thousands, even, of opportunities for fulfilling one's own destiny, for correcting errors by purging them with instructive pain and accumulated experience.

What is life, on man's long path of evolution? Nothing; barely a day, the lapse of time between the rising of the sun in the morning and its setting in the evening. Many lives of accumulating positive actions, like steps on the long evolutionary ascent, will lead us to complete the one and only Life.

THE STARS

"Infinite" is a concept that is too big for us. As our mind is not infinite, when it imagines something that is beyond it, it becomes overwhelmed, a shadow falls over it and it refuses to think.

But the infinite is there, just one step away, once we have left behind the secure and firm world of the earth, once we allow our gaze to wander across the heavens, through the stars, which are our points of reference in the depths of space. We know that mystery is great and unfathomable, but our infinite world is not a void; there are lights that shine here and there, and although they are situated at distances impossible to imagine, they serve as a point of support in the dizzying prospect of the outermost void.

Perhaps – as medieval people used to think – the stars are not lamps that God placed in the sky to give light to men. Science has already given its dry and definitive answer to that, and common sense indicates that God would not waste His energy creating worlds, just so that poor little human beings would not get lost in the night.

All that is true, but beyond that true logic, we feel that the stars are lights that Maya has lit in the universe as signs of life.

The stars, like us, are alive... but they are shining, they indicate their existence by allowing the light to pass through them, reflecting it intelligently, or vibrating in unsuspected ways and causing their atoms to transform speed into flashes of light.

Each glowing point that we see in the night sky is a beating life, a great, intelligent, conscious life, which is far more expansive than that of our poor, limited flesh, which needs a variety of subterfuges to avoid perishing in the darkness.

Maya is proud of the bodies of her stars, and that is why she lights them up every day, to the amazement and wonder of us human beings, who have not yet learnt to lose ourselves in the infinite.

***

Those tiny, shining points that appear in the sky are a proof of our own smallness. They are a wake-up call for the conceit of human beings, who believe they can dominate the universe with the few little machines they have learned to construct. It is not that human beings do not have the latent possibility to explore the universe, but it is not good to believe that we have already achieved it when we still don't know what it really means. It is not good to feel that we are masters when we have not yet ceased to be slaves.

What is the Earth – despite its innumerable interior mysteries, with its rocks, its plants, its animals and the human beings who inhabit it – beside those thousands of other worlds which glimmer in the mystery of the silence of night? We probably think the Earth is large, but what is this speck of dust in the form of a planet, in the midst of the infinite all around us?

It is essential that we know how to occupy our own place and know our own size, because only then can we begin to grow.

We no longer ask ourselves if there are other worlds, and if there is life on those worlds. By the simple evidence of our senses we know that there are other worlds, because we can see them. We know that they are alive and intelligent because the study of the few laws we have managed to discover prove that this is the case.

And it is most likely that those worlds are home to living beings, who are equal, inferior or superior to us. Why not? We cannot imagine a God so poor and limited as to have produced life only on this planet. Nor can we imagine that the human being is the only being worthy of living in the boundless infinite. Are we so perfect as to merit such a distinction?

Faced with these great mysteries, Maya plays with us with ideas of astronauts and extraterrestrials. Always focused on the material presence of things, we believe we are going to unveil the mystery because we can launch a few ships into space. We don't worry about whether the places we may find or the life-forms they may contain turn out to be superior to us, unless that superiority is expressed in technical systems more advanced than our own – which would be intolerable to our vanity.

Human beings are no longer interested in exploring their own planet; now they are more interested in setting out, not towards the mystery of the stars (who lives in the interior of those bodies?), but towards the conquest of outer space.

Sometimes Maya frightens us and makes us see "extraterrestrials" where there are no more than shadows and forms that are unknown to us. If we think a human being is a little crazier than others, we imagine we have found the fantastic inhabitant of another planet. And strangely enough, people are afraid of the inhabitants of those other planets. They always imagine them as being ugly, horrible, deformed in terms of our aesthetic criteria, but wise, superior and strong in relation to our knowledge. Even more than that: they are thought of as being cruel and hostile, and that their only aim is to enslave us in order to exploit us; might this perhaps be a psychological projection of what we would do to the inhabitants of another planet if we could subjugate them with our strength?

***

With all of this, Maya is hiding the true secret from us: the extraterrestrials are ourselves, who have two stars for our eyes and a restless soul within, which is looking at the infinite through the mirror of Maya.

TIME

Time is a form of energy, like space. Space is the dimension that is needed for bodies, whereas time applies to souls.

But Maya has trapped us in her game of material life and this is why, swept along by the game, we have also turned time into matter and apply it only to bodies. How long is a lifetime? How long does childhood last? How many hours do we need for rest? How much time should we spend on work? In order not to forget this increasing materialization of time, we have created some little memory devices that we wear on our wrists or carry in our pockets: watches, which measure each of our steps and show us how much 'time energy' we have used in taking them.

***

In spite of the satisfaction we may feel at having been able to measure time, we should be aware that we have not really achieved it. If we had, there would be no room for the distinctions we accept about the varying duration of time, whether we are referring to physical, psychological, mental or spiritual time. One hour measured by our watches is not the same as an hour of pain or an hour of joy; the hour of suffering is much longer than the hour of pleasure. An hour spent reading an interesting book passes by in a flash; an hour spent studying something we don't like seems eternal. An hour of spiritual expansion is infinitely brief; an hour of remorse and grief due to our low state of evolution can feel like a century...

That is why we have still not mastered the measurement of time. There are different types of hours and minutes, and not all of them can be captured by the same devices; moreover, time does not always affect us in the same way.

Chronological hours can enable us to become expert or knowledgeable in some subject over time. Whereas the hours of the soul are the only ones that can help us to evolve over many incarnations.

As in the case of so many other illusions, Maya has made us fear time, because she has made it seem synonymous with a destructive force that wears out and ages our bodies. And this is certainly true: old Chronos breaks us into little pieces day by day and places wrinkles on our skin for all to see.

But is this not also a veil? Is there not, behind this death and destruction, some special kind of transformation, of change that leads to evolution, of everlasting youth?

Sometimes we accept that it is good to change our skin, to leave behind our old clothes and renew the outer forms, so that the spirit can continue on its steady way through life. So, why are we afraid of changing our skin? Why do we weep over the bodies that get worn out? Is it not, perhaps, because we are afraid that the body we have may be the only one and, rather than a change of skin, represents a total loss of our one and only vehicle?

However, that is not how time works. Look at a tree: it doesn't think, and it feels more faintly than we do. It doesn't weep over its dead leaves; on the contrary, it rests throughout winter, content and bare of its leaves, with the certainty that it will awaken in the coming spring.

In the depths of all the changes that time brings about, there is no old age or death: there is eternal youth.

Youth is the heart of time: youth is not about lasting, it is about being.

***

A youthful person is one who keeps the skeleton of his existence unchanging, even if the skin that covers it may change its cells intermittently. He is one who has a single ideal always alive within him, who cultivates faithful feelings in his heart, who always acts in life in accordance with his thoughts, never ceasing in his action, whether in body, psyche or mind.

A youthful person is one who holds fast to the essential values because, as these values are very old, it is likely that the treasure of youth is also hidden within them; otherwise, they would not have been able to endure for so long.

***

Maya is perpetually young. We can only imagine illusion as an eternally youthful face. Maya is young because she works tirelessly in her game of life, always attentive to the interests that lead her to act.

Today, Maya has a special interest in the game of time that she applies to human beings. In her endlessly youthful spirit, in her attitude of never giving up, today she plays with our psychological world and influences it with a violent acceleration. Today, what used to take ten minutes can be done in one. Today, youth is shorter, adulthood is a gust of wind and old age arrives almost immediately. Things get worn out quickly; feelings disappear almost as soon as they arise and values roll in the hands of human beings like balls in a children's game.

What does this acceleration of time signify? Is it a form of evolution that is expressed as speed, or is it a kind of fall in which the speed of the descent exceeds the rhythm of the ascent?

***

Cycles are like the breath of time. With each motion of breathing in and breathing out, time builds and destroys civilizations.

Sometimes, time breathes slowly and calmly, at other times it does so quickly and convulsively. The calm breaths correspond to the happy periods of growth and construction, which can be seen in nations in general and human beings in particular. The hurried breaths correspond to the closing cycles of civilizations, where the old values fall and human beings barely manage to survive among the ruins, while at the same time dreaming of new and better times of ascending action.

Beyond the game of Maya, beyond her deceptive mirror in which things appear reversed, beyond all of that is eternal time, the pure energy in which those who have found their own inner eternity live: the ever-young, immortal Aphrodite of continuous consciousness.

OBEDIENCE

All the games of Maya have an appearance that we perceive through our senses and an essence that can be grasped by means of intelligent intuition. The appearance is the act of the game; the essence is the reason behind the game.

In view of this, obedience is the essence of the game that Maya presents to us under the form of freedom.

An old philosopher, one of those who managed to catch a glimpse of Maya's secrets, said that "freedom is conscious obedience to the law." And that's what it's about. These concepts that seem like opposites – freedom and obedience – are the soul and the body of one and the same entity.

***

All of us obey the great law of manifested existence, whether as a whole or through the many laws that emanated from it. But there are several ways of obeying. One of them is completely unconscious, although it seems that nothing in the world can restrain it; it obeys blindly, but believes that it is entirely free. At the other extreme, we find a conscious obedience, which tries to understand the meaning and purpose of the laws and abide by them in a healthy way.

Unconsciousness – which is not knowing, not understanding

– forces us into a strict obedience of the laws of matter, so that, whether we like it or not, we follow the classic rhythm of construction, preservation and destruction.

In this realm of unconsciousness, there are many who deem themselves "free", or even "liberated", but who dance to the rhythm that matter imposes on them. Although such people believe that they are choosing their actions, all they are doing is giving in to their sexual impulses (creation), to the desire to possess and accumulate (preservation), and to violence (destruction).

They are not free at all. They are not even free when they declare themselves to be free, because it is Maya who is speaking through their mouths, and it is she who is leading them back and forth, playing with the blindness that controls them.

Maya sings to them, sends them to sleep in her matter, and they obey her... in freedom.

As human beings gradually awaken, their blindness diminishes. Then the first possibilities of drawing back the veils of the game arise.

They see that the whole universe is governed by laws. The healthy need for observation arises, and the learned words and scholarly definitions are no longer as important as the simple contact with Nature, who teaches so much in each of her details.

From the small details comes the understanding of the law. From the recognition of the particular laws that govern each aspect of the universe, arises the conception that all of those small laws are contained within one great, total and general law, which embraces them all, unifying them and giving them meaning as a whole.

Now the game changes direction. Instead of obeying matter unconsciously, as we had done until now, the game consists in discovering the laws and intuiting the Law, and in making our being resonate with those systems of order that prevail in Nature.

Conscious obedience has been born.

***

Maya, who is free, knows how to make others obey. She is free because she herself absolutely obeys the laws of the game she directs. Having obeyed them herself, she obtains the right and the necessary skill to make human beings follow the same laws.

In her tremendous experience, Maya does not impose her rules; she gets human beings to accept them totally, especially those who consider themselves to be freer than anyone else.

Maya is gentle, attractive, smiling, affectionate, pleasing, lulling, deceitful, cunning, intelligent, demanding and apparently fickle... Who would not follow Maya, under these conditions? She imposes her law without imposing it. She simply leaves no other possible way for human beings. She knows everything about matter, while human beings are barely even starting to learn. That is why she commands and we obey her, though without realizing it.

There are very few human beings who can escape from this trap of illusion. Those few are able to disentangle themselves from the nets of Maya, which means that they have learnt whom, how and why they obey. With these few, Maya no longer plays so mercilessly; nor does she need to do so, because those few are consciously willing to obey her.

Those few who are conscious, who know what obedience is, continue to act in a similar way to other human beings; the difference lies in the fact that they know why they are acting as they do.

Freedom does not lie in the actions themselves, but in the consciousness that guides those actions. If human action is directed from outside, people cannot declare themselves to be free. If, on the other hand, action comes from within the human being, based on a clear awareness of the need for action, there is no need to declare oneself to be free.

One is already free. One is obedient. Just like Maya.

BEAUTY

Beauty is the harmonious presentation that Maya impresses on the forms of Nature. Once again we see that things assume an appearance so that they can be perceived by our senses. And every appearance induces us to search for the essence that lies behind it.

Behind the appearance of beauty there is an inner essence which, following Plato, we can call the Beautiful. This essence fills matter to a greater or lesser extent, impacting it and producing forms that are more, or less, harmonious. In some cases we speak of beautiful forms and, in others, of ugly or disagreeable forms.

Beauty, then, is the result of the touch that the Beautiful imposes on matter. If matter allows itself to be penetrated by that subtle, higher essence, then it becomes harmoniously moulded; and that charm which shines through it, even though it is matter, is beauty. If the essence of the Beautiful only touches matter weakly, the heaviness of the dense world prevails, and the aery and harmonious detail is lacking; in this case, there is a lack of beauty and we speak of ugliness.

***

The world of Maya is full of beauty. Despite the fact that she works with illusions, Maya uses beautiful illusions. All her elements are impregnated with harmony and all her acts obey a logical order.

Beauty is one of the supreme weapons with which Maya fights in the world of illusion; and it is a positive weapon, because with it she has won her greatest battles. Although human beings can resist strength, it is very difficult for them to resist beauty. The same human beings who don't find the motivation to get up and search for their own inner liberation are delighted, on the other hand, to run after the sinuous veils of Maya, the diffuse but suggestive lines, the soft perfumes, delicate melodies and dreamy colours.

Why do we run in that way after Maya, when she wields the weapon of her beauty? Once again we are moved by love, the need for something that we feel is absent. It is because we are looking for a form of harmony which we feel we have lost, which at that moment takes on the appearance of beauty. Maya has what we lack.

We, who almost always live as if we were asleep and walk with our eyes closed, nevertheless suspect that it is not enough for us just to keep our bodies in good shape, because we need a deeper beauty, a beauty that paints each of our gestures and actions, each word, each feeling, each idea, in a harmonious way.

Yet how we insist on maintaining the beauty of our bodies, as we fight with time to keep our figures and let out a desperate cry as we seek to capture the essence of beauty by fixing it in the most dense and certain thing that we human beings can conceive: matter.

***

There are two types of human beings who manage to escape from the game of Maya and no longer flirt with the attractive veils of her beauty: those who have freed themselves and see the essences beyond the forms, and those who are not yet fit to enter the game.

Taking for granted the fact that the great majority of human beings are engaged in Maya's games, we also do not need to consider the small number of those who have freed themselves from her games. But we would like to dedicate our reflections to the growing phenomenon of those who, being incapable of playing with beauty, denigrate it, making it dirty and disfiguring the forms of Nature.

These are the worshippers of ugliness. Fearful of Maya, rather than follow her laws, they prefer to ridicule them and, in order to do so, they punish the matter which she loves so much, by making their bodies ugly and exalting everything ridiculous and grotesque. They prefer the rough stone, unpolished and unmarked by intelligence, to the marvel of a finished and perfumed flower. And if they cannot find anything ugly enough to calm their thirst for destruction, they deform what they find, making it dirty and vulgar, breaking it into miserable fragments that do not even attain the illusory reality of Maya's beauty.

The cult of ugliness extends to bodies, clothes, meals that are eaten, gestures, words that are used, human relationships, something that claims to be art... And, above all, it permeates the look in people's eyes, eyes with the false brightness of animal malice, eyes without sensitivity, eyes that make us wonder whether we are truly in the presence of human beings.

How much easier it would have been to embrace the game of Maya, to let oneself just be in her arms, even unconsciously, and to grasp at least that source of beauty that animates her!

Poor, poor, helpless children who play hide and seek without taking the blindfold from their eyes to look for what they want! It is as if they think that what they don't see doesn't exist, and that is why they keep the blindfold on their eyes... Poor children of humanity who, as they don't see, don't walk: they only crawl and pick up rubbish from the ground, everything that those who are walking ahead have thrown away a long time ago!

But at some point Maya, playful as ever, will come to take off their blindfolds and cover their eyes with her veil of illusion, which is the beauty of life.

And the fact is that, in order to discover Maya and her beauty, one has to lift oneself out of the mud of the roads and learn to fly on the wings of her illusion. Whatever is heavy and ugly crashes to earth and is broken. What is beautiful attains the heights of eternity.

JUSTICE

When we look at the world around us, we can see how each thing has an appropriate place in which to develop, a place which is its own. This order, which is perceptible to the senses and the intelligence, has an essence, as we have mentioned on other occasions: it is 'the Just'.

When the essence of order, that is, the Just, is applied in the different circumstances of life, it gives rise to the different forms of justice. There can be many forms of justice, depending on the object they refer to; but the Just is one and universal.

***

Although a superficial analysis of the difficulties arising from matter might lead us to the conclusion that the world of Maya is evil and unjust, we must recognize in this case, as in all others, that Maya knows a lot about justice.

She is just towards herself, because she never gives herself more powers than those that are due to her according to her inner nature. And she is just towards others, since she does not play with human beings capriciously and never acts without a purpose.

If human beings believe that Maya is ambiguous and capricious, it is because they do not understand anything about the laws that rule her. The ambiguity with which she appears before us is due to a lack of knowledge on our part; her apparent whims are the forms in which our ignorance judges the variety of formulas that Maya has available to her.

All Maya's actions follow a remarkable logic; there is a reason for everything and it would be difficult for us to find solutions to life that are better and more well thought out than those that Maya applies. The whole of her world is imbued with logic, with order, and all the games that affect human beings, animals, plants, stones, stars and the infinite number of life forms that we are completely unaware of, are perfectly consistent with the cause that gave rise to them and the goal towards which they are moving.

This is the justice of the world of Maya, the Just applied to life.

***

Those who do not perceive the order of Nature do not attain happiness and assume that Justice does not exist.

These are the wilfully blind, those who live with their eyes closed and refuse to make the least effort to open them. But they are searching in the dark, bumping into one another frequently and encountering more difficulties than joys.

Everything looks grey, absurd and illogical to them... Nothing has any meaning, not even their own existence, which they carry around like a burden. But they will not listen to those who try to tell them about the meaning that life contains.

For these beings there is no justice, let alone the higher

essence that suffuses it and that we have defined as the Just. The world is an aggregation of irregularities and chance events, where a few human beings are favoured by good fortune to the detriment of others. Can we imagine any greater unhappiness?

Those who alter the order of Nature, claiming to do so in the name of justice, are criminals.

There is no lack of people who embody the saying "every law has its loophole". Such people do not doubt the order of Nature; but they study it patiently so that they can alter it and benefit personally from that change, at the expense of others, of course. These are the people who fill their mouths with the word "justice" and display it at every opportunity, as if the mere mention of the word would be sufficient to apply it. They are the ones who claim to know everything and have solutions for everything.

***

They are those who commiserate about human misfortunes, but whenever they do something to alleviate them, they profit a thousandfold more for themselves than what they give to others.

They try to make others see forms and colours that do not exist. They add new and heavier veils to the already natural veils of Maya, and in this way they make human life much more difficult. When human beings are at the mercy of the most terrible darkness, then they, the distorters, appear, to propose the saving "order", the order contrary to life, but favourable to their ambitions.

That is why we call them criminals. To be a criminal is not just to take someone's physical life. To take away their possibilities of evolution, to deceive them instead of educating them, to cheat them instead of helping them, is also an extremely serious crime. To attack Maya and her laws is a crime. To benefit from the pain of others is worse than a crime.

Those who look for justice in the disorder of anarchy, whether material or spiritual, are actually trying to avoid the natural work involved in living the order of justice.

The eternally lazy people, the ones who are comfortable in life, propose wonderful solutions, which are almost as criminal as those described above. For them, order is artificial, and things should be allowed to take their natural course. One should not interfere in anything, not direct anything, not intervene, not govern, not be governed.

It is true that things follow a natural course and, in any case, sooner or later – rather later than sooner – they would reach their destination. But the whole of Nature is full of examples in which the stronger leads the weaker, the higher rules the lower, light guides in the darkness. And it is in the mental nature of man to order the things that come within his control, because they belong to kingdoms below his own. Just as one can saddle a horse and arrange the furniture in a house, so one can arrange the circumstances of life to make them benefit the greatest possible number of beings.

If Nature is ordered and there are those who propose disorder, this is no longer following the "natural course of things"... It is quite the opposite.

It is very easy to want there to be no order when one is afraid that one will have to order oneself. It is easy to denigrate teachers when one does not want to learn. It is easy to refuse to obey when we don't have anyone to follow us and obey us...

What is difficult is to order oneself, to educate oneself, to obey; to know how to speak and to be silent at the right moment; to know how to see, to hear and to taste. In a word, to know how to live. Then, and only then, one can speak of justice.

***

How can we discover justice? Who can apply it?

Justice is discovered by the intelligent contemplation of Nature. Justice is discovered in the teachings and advice of those great beings who have existed in the world, those who knew how to work with Maya and revealed many of her secrets.

Someone who is able to see, who goes through life with open eyes, finds at each step the imprints of the Law, the footprint of the Just manifested in a justice that is necessary for life.

Human justice can only be applied by someone who has first achieved justice within himself, who has achieved an inner order in which the higher self prevails over the trivialities of the everyday personality.

How can we recognize such a person? Look at how they live; listen to what they say; see whether they act in accordance with their words; judge to what extent they are hard on themselves; and you will have found a rare example of a just man.

***

Justice, as it relates to our human life, is a harmonious sum of rights and duties. This has been said many times before, but it is appropriate to repeat it until it becomes firmly embedded in some part of our consciousness.

We all have rights. Maya grants us, in principle, the right to life with all its consequences. We all have duties. Maya demands of us that we fulfil the duties imposed on us by the human condition.

This harmony between what we can receive and what we must give makes up a whole, within the kaleidoscope of Maya, which is surprisingly similar to that other entrance door to Truth which we have called Beauty.

UNITY

One of the most important weapons that Maya plays with are her mirrors, which she places halfway between the higher world of spirit and the dense world of matter. These mirrors have the peculiarity of multiplying the spiritual unity, so that when the images are projected below, what was at first a single thing has been transformed into an infinite multiplicity, into thousands of attractive elements capable of enveloping human beings in their folds.

But behind the mirrors, behind the interplay of lights, is always unity.

While matter divides, spirit unifies. Maya, who acts in matter, is the divided reflection of the spiritual unity.

***

Only the human consciousness is capable of making the connection between the many things and unity. Consciousness ascends and descends, descends and ascends, constantly coming into contact with one pole of manifestation or the other.

When it descends, it finds Maya and her court of reflections arising from the division of the light. Then the consciousness also divides itself and plays at recognizing the various objects, trying to think about them and relate them together, looking for ways of making use of them and finding a meaning in them that it can relate to itself.

But when the consciousness ascends, it encounters the miracle of Maya which has also merged with the same unity that awaits us all, in that place where the games have come to an end, where experience is now complete, where the essence alone is the one and only reality.

***

The higher consciousness, the one that ascends, is the one that enables us to have a cosmovision. All things form part of a whole, a unity; all things lose what little particular value they had and gain the greater value of becoming part of that cosmic unity.

On the other hand, and in opposition to this consciousness, the other one, which turns its face towards matter, succumbs to separateness, a dangerous evil that can affect all the expressions of the human being.

Human beings become separated from one another, confront one another and fight against one another. All forms of union are overturned and, in a similar manner, the different religions and nations oppose one another. Political parties, trade unions and associations are created with the fundamental task of fighting with others of the same species. And the heights of separateness are reached in the confrontation that arises in the human being himself, when his two selves, the higher and the lower, lose all ability to live together and enter into war.

Separateness, then, is an evil of matter. If we give in to it and our consciousness falls prey to it, all living beings become divorced from one another before our eyes and we no longer find any link that can make an essential connection between them.

Unity is characteristic of the spirit. If the consciousness ascends to that plane, man finds his true root, his reason for being, and thereby immediately discovers an identical root in all things, and the essential connections between all of them become clear to him.

Everything depends, then, on our consciousness, and on placing it on one side or the other of the multiplying mirrors.

***

But Maya also plays with the consciousness and obliges it to oscillate between above and below. And in this case, we shouldn't forget that it is always easier to go down than to go up.

That is why we live in multiplicity, because we almost always find ourselves in a lower state of consciousness, down below, close to Maya and her games.

Our moments of becoming conscious of unity – of spirit – are sporadic. Let us take as an example a ball that falls down into a hollow: the speed of the fall to the bottom means that, once it has reached that point, it still has a little momentum to try to go up; but it doesn't have any elements to stabilize it in its ascent, and in this way Maya attracts it downwards again.

***

It is a question, then, of creating a higher home for our consciousness, a seat at the height of its possibilities, so that it will not fall again so easily. It is about placing a strong magnet on our point of unity, a light that focuses all the rays, a centre where all directions can converge; fixing oneself there with a new force of upward gravity – that of spirit – a force that is stronger and in the opposite direction to the force that Maya exercises over the world.

If we have learned to play below, if we have followed certain rules and an order to evolve among the many things, why should we not attempt a new stage? A stage in which the interest is focused on a higher game which brings together all things with the same meaning. Although she does not tell us, Maya is also dedicated to this same task, because at the end of it is the point where we will all meet.

GOOD AND EVIL

This is another of the great dualities that appear on the path of life, which Maya makes use of to carry on her game with human beings. Good at one pole, and evil at the other, allow room for a number of intermediate stages where things are not defined by either one extreme or the other, and it is there that the game is carried on; the game is no longer possible once one arrives at a final and definitive state.

Nevertheless, good and evil, as they are conceived by human beings, do not exist in an absolute form. They are just another illusory reflection of the mirrors of Maya; they exist in order to lead human beings from one point to another on the path of life, until we can discover by our own experience that destiny is not at one end or another, that extremes do not exist and that, as always, unity is the final result that lies beyond the dualities or multiplicities that we can perceive.

There is no absolute good; there is no absolute evil. How could two absolutes exist at the same time? How could the world be governed by two identical forces and in the opposite direction? By this criterion, God would be as powerful as the much feared devil, and the resolution of this opposition could never be achieved, since the two forces would balance each other out forever and ever. That is why today it is absurd is to conceive of an all-powerful Deity capable of combining all the powers of the universe.

***

From a human point of view – as we try to draw back slightly the veils of the game in which we are included – we can compare good with the polarity of spirit, and evil with the polarity of matter. Between the pole of spirit and that of matter there is room for infinite degrees of good and evil, giving rise to some half tones – the only ones we know – in which things are never fully defined.

And these are our constant questions. Is life good or bad? Is the mind positive or negative? Is money good or bad? Is it good to have pity or not? It all depends... Things in themselves are neither good nor bad. It is we who add those values to them, depending on whether we place them at one end or another of our scale, which goes from spirit to matter, from good to bad. If we were to colour the limits of our scale of values in white and black, we would find with sadness that, in truth, we do not know these pure shades and that we only work with an extensive range of lighter or darker greys.

***

But the dualities don't end here.

In the higher world of spirit, where we placed the realm of the good, there are also judgements. For spirit there are elements that are positive and others that are negative; there is a particular concept of what is good and what is bad.

Below, in the realm of matter, things are seen the other way around: good is what favours the game of Maya and bad is the opposite. Below, in this world where our consciousness spends most of its time, what is good is the variety of multiplicity, and even the anxiety that arises from not being able to choose between so much variety is seen as good. What is bad is what takes us out of this kaleidoscopic game; what is bad is what removes us from our innocent enjoyment of the objects of Maya, which we have come to believe in as the only possible reality.

The way human beings live – whether dedicated to the spiritual or the material aspect of life – determines how they develop their views of life. Hence the great disparity of opinions about good and evil, a divergence that corresponds to the disparity displayed by human beings in the evolutionary scale between matter and spirit.

In order to get human beings to agree on this subject, it would be necessary to promote a similarity in their aims, particularly as regards their evolution. And for now, with Maya present among us, this is very difficult. We will continue, then, for the moment, to fight for totally dissimilar goods and evils, which are sometimes opposites and at other times even include one another.

***

If for a moment we could overcome the illusion and see the common points of human ideas on the basis of the spiritual identity of all beings, then we would see that, in fact, there is no good or evil: only one thing exists, the Good, that which is at the same time the just and the necessary, the perfect and the eternal, what always is, beyond all the dualities through which it is reflected in the mirrors of Maya.

***

The Good emits a first reflection: goodness, which we have related to spirit. As this reflection descends, it expands, opens up and loses light, until it finally becomes darker as it reaches matter, the world of Maya, where it is transformed into evil. Maya, then, is the illusion that clouds the clear vision of the higher understanding. But, in order to balance this darkness, she has created a thousand artificial lights which, with the charm of their colours, play the part of goodness on the earth.

***

Should we deduce from all this that Maya is evil? Should we go back to attributing an absolute value to this world of illusion, making it appear as the worst of all possible things?

No, not at all. The darkness that comes from Maya and her resulting coloured lights are a necessary stage on the path.

If we did not live enshrouded by mist, we would never have an intuition of, or long for, clarity. Through darkness we come to the light. Through matter we glimpse the spirit. Through the interplay of multiplicities we dream of the certainty of a single and final goal.

PHILOSOPHY: ARIADNE'S THREAD

At the dawn of classical Greece, there was a myth rich in deep meanings, which represented several of the mysteries of life: it was the story of the Minotaur, an indefinable monster that dwelt in the centre of a complex labyrinth and inexorably "swallowed" anyone who attempted to capture it. Nevertheless, one man emerged – Theseus – who, helped by the image of his own soul – Ariadne – was able to reach the centre of the mystery, master the monster and return victorious through the multiple paths of the labyrinth.

What was the key to Theseus's success? It was a spindle with a long coil of thread, which Ariadne gave him before he entered the labyrinth; the thread unrolled as the hero walked into the depths of the cave and enabled him to recognize the path of return.

That is why we have called philosophy "Ariadne's Thread", the key that leads us to discover the mysteries of the world of Maya.

***

Maya, with her games, has created a veritable labyrinth in life, with intricate paths that never appear clearly to the eyes of human beings. In this way, they play like children, trying out a thousand and one paths to enable them to reach, either the mystery – the centre – or the exit.

Although the games of Maya and her labyrinth might seem evil at first glance, we have to recognize once again the intelligence with which illusion operates, so that, at some point, once we have overcome all the obstacles – all the games – we can gain the secret that lies at the axis of the heart of the cave.

Meanwhile, Maya possesses an immense power that enables her to trap human beings in her twists and turns, since almost no one knows the way out. In this way, we are all trapped by material life, because almost no one knows the way out of this prison. And as we cannot escape, would it not be best to try to play inside it, going round and round, until the soul offers us a saving thread?

***

The labyrinth contains two great secrets: one, the easiest to discover, is the solution to the problem of finding the way out; the other, which is a more profound secret, is that which lies at the centre of its many paths. There is no possibility of getting out until we have mastered the monster. There is no possibility of resolving the problems of life until we have understood the enigma of the games of Maya. In this way, the most important of all secrets is the one that sleeps in its heart; without the brave souls who dare to face the Minotaur, there will be no brave souls who can escape from the labyrinth.

If philosophy – the love of wisdom – is Ariadne's Thread, it is by following her tracks that we will be able to reach the hidden place where Maya has her root: philosophers are the ones who search, who have conquered the fear that characterizes ignorance, who want to know the reason behind her games, even as they continue to play.

Theseus with his ball of wool, Ares Dionysus with his axe-torch, the ordinary human being with the lamp of his intelligence, all are seekers and lovers of wisdom, they are philosophers. By entering boldly onto the paths of existence, they come ever closer to the centre and there, where the great monster should be, they discover – oh surprise! – the dwelling of Maya, the great illusion that rules the games of the labyrinth. The games always lead to the heart of the labyrinth, as if they were interconnected trials: if human beings arrive there blindly, the monster of illusion devours them; if they arrive with a longing to know, the monster lets its veils fall and Maya appears in all her splendour as the great ruler of human experiences.

To have discovered Maya and her veils, to have understood the reason behind her games, is to have reached wisdom. Then, even if one is at the very centre of the labyrinth, it is as if one were at the exit; the secret of the centre is the secret of liberation.

***

That is why Maya has covered philosophy with veils. Instead of allowing us to know it in its simplicity and purity, in its simplicity as a guiding thread, she has overburdened it with excessive words, deceptive images, an infinite number of definitions, technicalities, expressions of doubt and anguish, raising hundreds of problems with no solutions. Maya needs human beings in her labyrinth and that is why she opens multiple paths for them, which, just as in children's games, lead nowhere.

***

However, from time to time, as a result of wandering along those paths, there are human beings who reach the monster, there are those who decipher the mystery of the Minotaur, there are heroes who have patiently wound their knowledge around a saving spindle.

For these human beings who have reached wisdom through philosophy, knowledge is power. Someone who knows what is happening in the heart of the labyrinth can escape. Someone who finally emerges from the world of Maya does not do so only for his own liberation. Just like Theseus, he escapes in order to warn other human beings, to teach them and help them avoid greater sorrows in the difficult period that results from living with a body, giving in to its needs, playing with its laws...

***

The labyrinthine world of Maya is not a false or malicious world, nor is it opposed to the world of truth. It is a faint reflection of those other higher worlds, and as a reflection it traps everything that it can in its dim lights and in its matter slowed down by its weight. The world of Maya complies with her law and most of the time we human beings distort its images even more, as a result of our poor vision. To play does not mean to do so as if we were asleep; to play does not necessarily imply closing our eyes when we do so. To play does not force us to be unconscious of what we are doing: rather, it demands that we know why we are doing it.

Philosophy, then, gives us that clarity of vision and understanding that the blindness of inertia has caused to disappear in human beings.

Philosophy is recognition: to "re-cognize", to rediscover what belongs to the soul and has become lost by playing. It is the solution to the mystery of the labyrinth, it is the triumphal departure towards the world of real beings, towards the world of the primary archetypes whose images had accompanied us for so long.

Maya has allowed herself to be conquered by Theseus. She herself is the conqueror of herself, since she has created the great illusion in order to allow herself to be known by those who, beyond the shadows, have discovered her true form.

GOD

Maya: those who do not know you very well say that you have tried to hide the root of existence from the eyes of men, that you have attempted by all means to keep them blind in ignorance, so that in this way you can play with them better. They say all those things about you, Maya...

And yet, you have developed an excellent formula for achieving quite the opposite of what is attributed to you. It is true that you play, it is true that you lay fine nets to trap human beings in the illusory world of matter; it is true that you prefer the continuity of the wheel of life to the final liberation, because you live with those who are living. All of that is true, but you do not deny God, nor do you hide Him any more than you hide any other truth.

Each of your steps, every bend in the road, every game, every nuance of light and shade, is an invitation to question, to search for the reason behind things. It is like that child whom I described at the beginning of these thoughts, who played while knowing that he was playing, although without ceasing to play.

You repeat your laws unceasingly, ensuring that, by dint of always going back over the same steps, we may at some point ask ourselves where those steps are leading.

Who is directing the game? Maya.

And who is directing Maya? God.

God is the root of existence. Manifested existence implies an interplay of values until an equilibrium emerges from the duality and one can return to the root. Maya is the one who coordinates the game, but once it has come to an end, she too will return to the bosom of mystery together with all those who have been victorious in life.

***

God: in the game of life you have been given so many names, and human beings have fought over your names. They have given you so many forms, and they have fought hard battles to impose one of your appearances over the others. They have given you so many attributes, and human beings still continue to argue about the qualities which supposedly adorn you, forgetting that for each quality they give you, there are so many more that they take away... forgetting that you are absolute and that everything is a part of you.

God: thousands of philosophical writings, arguments and doctrines have been dedicated to you. The best poems have been written in your name. Books and words about you have filled history and continue to do so.

What can I give you?

Beyond all the games, beyond all the intellectual judgements,

I cannot find a better name for you than the one you have: God. And I can only offer you my devotion in the form of works. That is my intention, I leave you to be the judge.

EPILOGUE

To end these thoughts, we can go back to the words with which this book began and repeat what was said at the beginning: Maya is illusion.

But what exactly is this illusion? Is it non-existence? Is it a falsehood? It is not a falsehood, because – whether or not it is an illusion – it exists; nor is it non-existent, because this perpetual game is taking place for all living beings. Maya exists, she is real: she fulfils a real function, which is to teach us about false and non-existent things... about those things that are like a brief flash of light, like dust beside the great existence, beside the great Truth.

Maya is a mirror. She is neither good nor bad; she does not inhabit the world of absolute archetypes, nor does she share the fleeting nature of material bodies. She is in the centre, working as an intermediary between the two worlds.

On one side of the mirror – let us call it the lower pole – are moving shadows that are very similar to the true beings, shadows that have all the appearance of reality.

These reflections are not real, even though they appear to be; they merely repeat those things which are real. But the truth can still be deduced from the inverted reflections in the mirror, just as when we ourselves are reflected in a mirror and it enables us to become aware of our appearance – even if it is inverted.

The shadows reflected by Maya are constantly moving.

How real is movement? To which side of the mirror does it belong?

Movement is characteristic of multiplicity and is, therefore, on this side of things. On the other side of the mirror things do not move... they simply are.

However, through the game of movement, we can learn about non-movement, by inverting the images.

Although movement takes place between the many bodies, the phenomenon is not produced by the force of matter; it is the will that brings matter into play. Matter alone, by its mere multiplicity, cannot move, but it can give rise to the phenomenon of movement if the will sets it in motion.

If it is the will that makes the living machine function, then there is unity. The will is the only force that comes from the other side of the mirror, passes through it and is transformed into movement in our everyday world.

Thus, from unity, from the only existing point, arises the illusion of movement and of the reproduced bodies, once again thanks to the changing reflections in the mirror of Maya.

***

If we accept movement, we can now ask ourselves: What are we moving towards? Where are we going?

Although we are not able to see clearly the direction of the path or where it is leading, we can explain our movement along the path with a simple idea: evolution.

Evolution is the force that the will or spirit has interwoven into the material shadows, so that, at some point, they will be able to free themselves from the net of Maya and pass to the other side of the mirror.

When this happens, the rhythm of the games, the net, the mirror – all of that will have ceased to be necessary. Maya herself will have fulfilled her role and will be reintegrated into the world of pure ideas; she too will have purified her body of multicoloured glass by evolution.

But now is not yet the time. We are still immersed in the games of Maya. Now we have to learn by playing and learn, day by day, to perfect the role which this game has allotted to us.

That is why we say: 'Welcome Maya.'

'Welcome, Teacher!'

ABOUT THE AUTHOR

Delia Steinberg Guzmán was born in Buenos Aires (Argentina) on 7th January 1943. In 1972, she moved to Madrid (Spain) and was granted Spanish nationality in 1975.

She had a degree in Philosophy from the University of Buenos Aires and graduated from the National Conservatory of Music in Buenos Aires as a Teacher of Piano and Composition. In 1982, she founded the piano competition which, since 2008, has been known in the musical world as the Delia Steinberg International Piano Competition. The competition is a member of the Alink-Argerich Foundation.

From 1972 to 1991 she was the Director of New Acropolis (Nueva Acrópolis) in Spain, during which time she expanded the cultural activity of this institution to more than 30 cities around the country. She has also coordinated the activities of New Acropolis in Europe.

After the death of the founder, Jorge Ángel Livraga, in 1991, she was elected International President of New Acropolis. In this capacity until 2020, she was responsible for managing and coordinating the cultural and educational work of New Acropolis in all the countries in which this international association is established. Thereafter, she served as the Honorary President of the International Organization New Acropolis until her death in August 2023.

She has written more than thirty books and handbooks about Practical Philosophy, Psychology, Ancient Civilizations, Astrology, etc., including the following:

The Everyday Hero (NA. Mumbai, 2018)
Philosophy for Living (NA. Mumbai, 2016)
What do we do with the Heart and the Mind? (NA. Bangalore, 2019)
Para Conocerse Mejor (Know Yourself Better) (Editorial NA. Madrid, 2015).
El Ideal Secreto de los Templarios (The Secret Ideal of the Templars) (Editorial NA. Madrid, 2015).
Several of her works have been translated into other languages in over 40 countries.

NEW ACROPOLIS

INTERNATIONAL ORGANIZATION NEW ACROPOLIS

New Acropolis is a worldwide non-profit organization, with centres in over fifty countries.

Established by Professor Jorge Angel Livraga on the foundations of practical philosophy and universal fraternity, New Acropolis is inspired by a fundamental respect for human dignity beyond differences of race, gender, culture, religion or socio-economic status. New Acropolis respects diversity but also tries to transcend it in search of a higher unity through shared universal ethical principles.

At New Acropolis, philosophy is more than just intellectual food for thought. We study philosophy as a means to integrate science, arts, ethics and metaphysics in order to work towards global human development.

This vision is implemented through a wide range of programs that combine practical education with cultural and volunteering activities. New Acropolis also promotes an awareness of current affairs, both locally and globally and focuses on improving the human condition by aligning ourselves with the laws of nature.

To learn more about New Acropolis, visit www.acropolis.org